I0616346

Ordering Information:

Quantity sales. Special discounts are available on quantity purchases by corporations, associations, and others. For details, contact the publisher at the address above.

Orders by U.S. trade bookstores and wholesalers. Please contact keiperg2018@gmail.com

Printed in the United States of America

First Printing, 2021

ISBN: 978-1-63630-701-5 (paperback)

Second Edition:

ISBN 979-8-218-18777-4 (paperback)

ISBN 979-8-218-18778-1 (eBook)

8 WEEKS OF REFLECTIONS WITH GOD

His Welcoming Arms

A daily prayer study guide

GLENDA KEIPER

To Kricky
One day, we shall dance again.

&

To my Aunt Ouida whose prayers
protected my life.

TABLE OF CONTENTS

HIS WELCOMING ARMS
GLENDA KEIPER

TABLE OF CONTENTS

A DAILY PRAYER STUDY GUIDE

TABLE OF CONTENTS

Beginning

Are you standing on the edge of a new experience? Whether you're filled with trepidation, excitement, or both, a new, emotional adventure with God awaits you. We all want to find out more about God and His Word, but ask yourself, "Do I want to change my life?" There's a fear we all have at some point where we worry if we're going to be enveloped and comforted by God's message, or find condemnation.

I was once standing where you are. I had no idea, really, about the Bible, nor did I know anything about having a relationship with God. I wasn't raised going to church. Oh, I knew many of the Bible stories, but as an adult, I had no idea about what else the Bible had to say.

In my twenties, my best friend joined a church and started a small study group. The Bible study was specifically for those who didn't know God. It was led by loving, mature

Christian women who taught me about what it was to know God. My knowledge about God and His Word grew week by week, as I learned about salvation and how to pray. I learned the difference between the children's stories I had learned and the depth of God's love.

His Welcoming Arms

There's one thing to always remember when it comes to God, His arms are wide and welcoming. He is evident in our daily lives; if we want to know Him. To me, God's Word is always fresh. Each day it speaks to me on a personal level.

In this daily devotional, I hope to share with you what I know of God's love and how it has changed my life and continues to change me. More than anything, I hope that it will encourage you.

For me, being new to church was like starting out at a new school without the scent of a freshly waxed floor. I didn't know the people or the materials. What was the Bible about? Where should I start? How does everyone know all these scriptures? Wait... do I have to memorize all the scripture? There were so many important questions and my mind began to spiral. Let's talk about these questions.

What Does the Bible Consist of?

The Bible consists of several types of literature within the Old and New Testaments. The Old Testament recounts the story of creation and the religious life of the Jewish people. The Old Testament follows the lineage of Christ from Adam and Eve to before the birth of Christ. It contains prophecies about the coming of the Messiah, the one who would liberate the Jewish people. The New Testament is the fulfillment of the Old Testament's prophecies. It is the record of Jesus, his birth, life, and ministry. It recounts his crucifixion and resurrection; the sacrifice he made for the sins of all.

Where Do I Start?

Right where you are. God doesn't expect you to come to Him knowing everything. He loves you where you are and delights in you wanting to learn more about Him. Allow the Holy Spirit to teach and guide you (John 14:26).

How Does Everyone Know All These Scriptures?

I wanted to know the same thing! And the answers vary. Some people were raised in the church. They learned to memorize scripture in Sunday school. Others simply enjoy having verses memorized so that they don't have to look them up. Every person has a different story.

Do I Have to Memorize a Bunch of Scriptures?

Nope. We have the Bible, the Living Word of God, as a resource. Although you may want to memorize those scriptures that have special meaning for you.

Spending time reading the Word each day and determining how God is speaking to you through scripture is the best way to grow as a Christian and develop your relationship with God. You desire spending time with loved ones, and God desires to spend time with you. Why else would He have provided a way for us to come to Him?

Do I Have to Give Up Things I Enjoy Doing?

Some things are definitely sinful. You can't murder, steal, commit adultery, worship idols, or violate any of the Ten Commandments. While other acts aren't sins per se, they can become sinful. Dancing isn't sinful, but it could be if it promotes lewd behavior and tempts others into sexual immorality. Smoking isn't listed as a sin, but it does destroy the body, which is a temple of the Holy Spirit (1 Cor. 6:19). Let God lead you. Learn to listen to what the Holy Spirit is saying to your heart.

What is a Christian?

A Christian believes that there is one God, who gave His only Son as a sacrifice for our sins so that whoever believes in Him would not perish but have life everlasting. A Christian believes that Jesus Christ was born through a virgin birth, lived, died, and was resurrected on the third day. It is the belief that because of the sin of Adam and Eve, humans had a broken relationship with God, which through Jesus was made whole. Christians believe in a three-in-one God: God the Father, Jesus the Son, and the Holy Spirit.

What Does it Mean to Have a Relationship With God?

God already loves us. This relationship will build as we learn about Him. The growth in understanding Him and His purpose for us brings richness to the relationship. Spending time in prayer and learning what the Scriptures say is the beginning of that understanding.

Being new to prayer can be daunting. There is no right or wrong way to pray. Prayer is a holy conversation between you and God, your heavenly Father. It can be as formal or informal as you are comfortable with.

I found that for me it starts in His Word. The Holy Spirit is faithful to show us whatever we seek. He works in wisdom and knowledge and love. He convicts, but never condemns. His corrections are gentle, but not demeaning. If you want to increase your faith and grow closer to God, there is no better way to start than to take a journey with Him through scripture.

What Bible Should I Use?

If you are unfamiliar with the Bible or don't have one, I recommend the YouVersion Bible app. It is free and has a multitude of versions and languages. You can read two different versions side by side for comparison. It also has an audio feature so you can listen as you drive or work. I rely on the search feature to quickly find verses.

Before you purchase a Bible, it is for you to decide which version you like. My first Bible was an NIV (New International Version) Study Bible, which had notes about how the verses related to other verses. The one I have now is an NRSV (New Revised Standard Version) Cultural Bible, which provides information about the culture at the time and place a book was written. Growing up, we had the King James Version, which has lovely poetic languag but uses a form of English that is no longer used in everyday communication.

The new versions, such as the Message and others, have contemporary language that is easier to understand.

How to Use This Book

This book is designed to be used in three different ways. You may use it as a personal prayer diary recording your prayer each day; cultivating a habit of talking to God. Or, as a daily devotional to nurture your relationship with God. This book may also be used in a group study. In this atmosphere, the weekly review questions will help to facilitate discussion about your experiences, as well as those of others.

Questions for consideration have been added at the end of each week. This will help you review what you have discovered during the week. I have included the daily scripture with each reading, but you may want to look it up in a different version to increase your understanding or comfort. There is a page at the end of each week to write thoughts and questions.

All references to Scripture are from the NIV unless otherwise noted.

My Spiritual Goals

What do you hope to gain spiritually from reading this devotional?

_____

_____

_____

_____

_____

_____

_____

_____

_____

_____

_____

_____

_____

_____

_____

_____

_____

_____

_____

_____

_____

_____

The God Who Loves Us

Week 1

Day 1

God Knows Your Heart

For God so loved the world that he gave his only Son, [Jesus Christ], that whosoever believes in Him shall not perish but have life everlasting.
(John 3:16 NIV)

We are often without the words to pray for ourselves or others. Starting with a verse and asking God to teach you its meaning, is one of the most effective ways to start learning the truths found within the Bible. Try reading it several times to expand upon it. I might look up the meaning of words and see if substituting another word helps the scripture bring clarity to my current situation. When reading a scripture, ask the Holy Spirit to show you how it applies to your life.

Let's start with John 3:16. Yes, the one you see on the eyelids and cheeks of sports stars, and on signs held by fans. It is usually the first verse that anyone learns. It's no wonder this is the most advertised verse of the Bible—it's the story of Jesus in a nutshell. It teaches us that God loved us so much that He provided a way for us to have a relationship with Him.

Genesis, the first book in the Old Testament, starts with the story of creation. In the beginning, God created Adam and Eve, two people that He walked with in the Garden of Eden (Gen. 3:8). When Adam and Eve sinned, they were cast out of the garden. That sinful nature separated all of mankind from God in the New Testament, we see the story of how God provided his Son, through a virgin birth, to be the way to our salvation. We are saved from eternal death and given eternal life. The life, death and, resurrection of Jesus opened the door for all of us to have a relationship with the living God. This gift of love was freely given, an act of grace.

John 3:16 is a great starting point for your communication with God. Your prayers can be as long or short, as detailed or concise as you feel led; but the important thing is to open the conversation. God knows your heart and will love you through it.

Reflection & Prayer

My prayer:
Father, thank You that Your hand is upon me. Thank You for loving me so much that just my belief in Jesus gives me the promise of eternal life. I could never earn this gift of Your love. You in Your grace, mercy, and love, provided a way through Jesus Christ for me to be able to come before You. Thank You for that salvation. Amen.

Your Prayer:

_____

_____

_____

_____

_____

_____

_____

_____

_____

_____

Question to Consider:

How does today's verse help you understand the relationship that we have with God?

_____

_____

_____

_____

_____

_____

_____

_____

_____

_____

_____

_____

_____

_____

_____

_____

Day 2

God's Word

All Scripture is God-breathed and is useful for teaching, rebuking, correcting and training in righteousness.
(2 Timothy 3:16 NIV)

"All Scripture is God-breathed," this is how we know that we can trust Scripture. It was written by man, but God gave each author the wisdom and words He wanted used to record His story. Whether in the Old Testament or the New, God inspired the authors of the various books of the Bible.

Take great comfort in the fact that he used ordinary men to accomplish this. Throughout the Bible, God used people whose sins were evident: Moses and Paul were murderers, Rahab was a prostitute, Abraham was a liar, David committed adultery, and Jacob was a swindler. All of these people were used in mighty ways by God despite their sinful nature. God had a purpose for each to bring glory to His name, just as He has a purpose for you.

When we read God's Word every day, it speaks to our hearts. As we go through this study, we will learn about God and what he wants from our lives. Think about this and how it makes you feel.

Personally, I have been rebuked by what I have read in Scripture. A seemingly innocent verse will speak to my heart, showing me how my thought or action is incorrect, just as a parent corrects a child. And each and every correction is done for a purpose to show me ways that I could draw closer to God.

God's Word isn't for condemnation. I get so upset by pastors that use God's Word to shame people into living differently. Yes, some sins anger God but look at the words used in the scripture above: "rebuking and correcting" are not condemnation. They are not full of anger. They are loving, welcoming us into His presence, and telling us how the Holy Spirit will guide us to live a life of righteousness.

Reflection & Prayer

My prayer:
Father, thank You that You love us so much that You provide a way for me to draw closer to You. You offer gentle correction, showing me a better way, not just telling me what I did wrong. Please guide me today. Amen.

Your Prayer:

_____

_____

_____

_____

_____

_____

_____

_____

_____

_____

_____

_____

Question to Consider:

How does this day change the way that you think about Scripture?

_____

_____

_____

_____

_____

_____

_____

_____

_____

_____

_____

_____

_____

_____

_____

_____

Day 3

Lift Your Burden

If we confess our sins, he is faithful and just and will forgive us our sins and purify us from all unrighteousness
(1 John 1:9 NIV)

Confession is the tough part. For with confession comes the admission that we were aware of the wrongness of our actions. God already knows about it, but He wants us to admit that we know about it. Why?

As a parent, there were many times that I knew one of my daughters had done something wrong. I wanted them to tell me so that I was assured that they understood the wrongness of their action. It was important so that they could grasp how their actions affected others. The apology was essential to remove the offense from standing between us. When needed, it is important to offer a true apology, not an

11

off-the-cuff "Sorry" that means nothing. A true apology starts with "I am sorry," includes the offense, and ends with "Please forgive me." It shows a tenderness of the offender's heart to the person who was injured. It shows sincerity.

Not all actions are directed toward others. Many of our sins hurt us by grieving the Holy Spirit. When we sin by breaking a Commandment, such as envying another or lusting after someone other than our spouse, we are driving a wedge between us and our loving God. The longer the sin is ignored, the more callused the heart becomes. By apologizing, the act can be forgiven and then forgotten. It isn't left hanging, niggling at either party like a guilty pain, never being allowed to heal. Unrepentance left to fester breeds arrogance in the offender, and anger in the offended. The longer we remain unrepentant, the harder it becomes to ask forgiveness. God the Father wants to forgive us. He wants to know that we understand how an action was wrong and who it hurt. When this happens, we can confess it immediately and be done with it. We are free to forgive ourselves. After confession and repentance, God looks and there is nothing there. God has forgotten it. We can continue to haul it around as long as we want, but God no longer sees it.

Reflection & Prayer

My prayer:
Thank You, Father, for Your Son, who came to open the way for us to come to You. Forgive me, Lord, for the hurts that I have caused. Show me, Lord, who is still in pain from one of my actions. If I am unable to apologize to them, please heal their hearts of the pain, Lord. Forgive me for the pain I have caused. Forgive me for indulging in the actions that I know bring sorrow to You. Remove the hardness from my heart that I may be ever more aware of You. Amen.

Your Prayer:

_____

_____

_____

_____

_____

_____

_____

_____

_____

_____

Question to Consider:

Is there something that has been forgiven by God, that you need to forgive yourself for so that it may be forgotten?

_____

_____

_____

_____

_____

_____

_____

_____

_____

_____

_____

_____

_____

_____

_____

_____

_____

Day 4

Freedom of Choice

"The Lord God took the man and put him in the Garden of Eden to work it and take care of it. And the Lord God commanded the man, "You are free to eat from any tree in the garden; but you must not eat from the tree of the knowledge of good and evil, for when you eat from it you will certainly die."

(Genesis 2:15–17 NIV)

"Now the serpent was more crafty than any of the wild animals the Lord God had made. He said to the woman, "Did God really say, 'You must not eat from any tree in the garden'?" The woman said to the serpent, "We may eat fruit from the trees in the garden, but God did say, 'You must not eat fruit from the tree that is in the middle of the garden, and you must not touch it, or you will die.'"

"You will not certainly die," the serpent said to the woman. "For God knows that when you eat from it your eyes will be opened, and you will be like God, knowing good and evil."

(Genesis 3:1–5 NIV)

In this creation account, Adam is given the garden of Eden to tend to. One rule was put in place: do not eat from the tree of knowledge of good and evil. Why do you suppose that God put one restriction on Adam? Why put the tree there at all if he didn't want Adam to eat from it?

It isn't that God wanted Adam to sin, but Adam was created with free will. How else could he demonstrate his love for God? With the choice to obey or disobey, God would know whether Adam wanted to obey him out of a desire to please him or not.

I wonder what Adam knew of death. The Earth and Adam were new creations. No death had entered the garden. God created Eve, and they lived in the garden until the serpent had a conversation with Eve. He was right, physical death wouldn't be immediate, but the death of innocence would be. The serpent neglected to mention the consequences of knowledge, for with the knowledge of good and evil would come the knowledge of death. Until this moment, they were allowed to eat from the tree of life but with knowledge came a new restriction: they would no longer live as long as God (Gen. 3:22–23). They were sent from the garden to live a harsher existence dependent upon their labors in the land. Now they would need to kill animals, and one of their sons would kill the other— all consequences of their knowledge of good and evil.

How often are we duped by partial truths? The serpent did not mention that with knowledge came sadness, shame, anger, bitterness, and all the negative emotions that would be revealed. When a friend shares hurtful information about another, it is painful. We may be embarrassed or angry when previously, we had been innocent of the knowledge. Now our view of the other person has changed.

16

I can't imagine the loneliness Adam and Eve must have experienced by being cast out of God's presence. To have been able to walk in a lovely garden with Him and then to be exiled to a world without His presence with them must have been devastating. I wonder if Adam had bitterness toward Eve. Did he hold a grudge? Did they quarrel over their new circumstances? So much changed in one moment.

Reflection & Prayer

My prayer:
Lord, You gave us free will. I have the freedom to choose
what I want to do every day. I can choose to follow You or
choose to pursue the ways of the world. Please help me to
make good choices today. Amen.

Your Prayer:

_____

_____

_____

_____

_____

_____

_____

_____

_____

_____

_____

_____

_____

_____

Question to Consider:

In what way does this change the way you think about God?

_____

_____

_____

_____

_____

_____

_____

_____

_____

_____

_____

_____

_____

_____

_____

_____

Day 5

The Action of Faith

And without faith it is impossible to please God, because anyone who comes to him must believe that he exists and that he rewards those who earnestly seek him.

(Hebrews 11:6 NIV)

According to the Bible Dictionary, "Faith is a spiritual attitude involving action." I rarely think of faith as a verb. I think of faith as a noun— something I have or want more of, wondering to myself, "Do I portray enough peace, confidence, and joy when it comes to God?" Faith in action is many things. Every one of us has a unique gift or calling if you will. Faith is evident in the workplace by the way you speak and interact.

When I worked in the business world, the "church ladies" were my special group of clients. Their computer aptitude was usually low and required a ton of patience, but their

21

love and faith shone through. I loved working with them so much that when I went to a new product, I told the manager that I would take all the church ladies (just don't give me the demanding business folks). Nope, give me a church lady every day of the week, and I will try to pray for the others!

See, it was the business people that wanted no part in doing their own work. They didn't want to learn or to talk kindly to others. Faith through action can be just as important as the internal emotions that come with faith.

Faith is also strength and confidence. When others are worrying or anxious, faith anchors us. Our confidence in the ability of God is evident to others. Our God is our strength and confidence. When you know that, you will know that God is able, that God is faithful, and that God loves you. It becomes apparent that you have inner peace, a knowledge that you need not give in to fear.

Today, what does my faith show? Does it show growth, love, and acceptance of others? Would it please the Lord for people to associate me as one of His? Does my faith produce an action that draws others in or scares them off? The action of faith is visible in what we do and how we live our lives. By living and breathing your faith, you are modeling it through your actions. Others can simply see your faith without you ever having to speak on it. Faith is modeled by your trust in God, and this in turn pleases Him.

Reflection & Prayer

My prayer:
Father, my faith in You is my security. You are in every ray of sunshine and every drop of rain. Your name is rustling in leaves and roaring in the wind. Build my faith, Father. Let it be a beacon for others, pointing them to Your love and mercy. You are constant in a world that is full of chaos. Your peace pervades my being, pushing aside fear. "Great is thy faithfulness, Lord, unto me." Amen.

Your Prayer:

_____

_____

_____

_____

_____

_____

_____

_____

_____

_____

Glenda Keiper

Question to Consider:

What are your questions related to faith?

_____
_____
_____
_____
_____
_____
_____
_____
_____
_____
_____
_____
_____
_____
_____
_____

Day 6

Loving Guidance

Search me, God and know my heart; test me and know my anxious thoughts. See if there is any offensive way in me, and lead me in the way everlasting.
(Psalms 139:23, 24 NIV)

As much as I know in my mind that the Lord is with me always, it is a different matter to ask Him to go with me on a tour of my heart. I know what is in there—all of the junk of the day, the week, the past ten years. All of the darkness in the corner of my heart that I am ashamed of. All those moments of triumph over others. The last hurtful word, or action that I knew made others angry or caused pain. The denial that caused someone else a punishment. Even unintentional hurts that my pride stopped me from apologizing for. Whether intentional or unintentional, whether a "small lie" or a whopper, it is all the same in God's eyes. And that can be terrifying when we go to Him.

"Know my anxious thoughts." I am not one to speak in front of crowds, and yet I once accepted a job as a trainer. My class sizes ranged from six to twenty. I was called on to speak in front of large groups. Talk about anxious. I would get so nervous that I would prepare what I wanted other people to say! But each and every time I talked to God and asked for His help, I walked in confidently. The times I forgot to pray were the times that I was conscious of the crowd and hesitant.

It's important to recognize ways that are offensive to God. There are times when we get angry or hurt. Our pride can make us unwilling to let it go. When we hold on to an offense, even though we know that God wants us to forgive, we create unneeded clutter and pain that could otherwise be avoided. If we don't share the whole truth about something because it puts our actions in a bad light we only hold onto that darkness longer. Do not fear the wrath of God, but take joy in His forgiveness and love.

The Holy Spirit is faithful to show us whatever we seek. He works in wisdom and knowledge and love. He convicts but never condemns. His corrections are gentle and not demeaning. It is a daring move to prayerfully ask God to know our anxious thoughts because of what it might uncover in our hearts. But there is no danger. God will lovingly offer correction and solace. He will show you ways to open your heart to learn His ways. You will be lovingly guided through pain, fear, and resentment. He will comfort you. When we trust God to examine our hearts, we can say "Stop" when we have gone as far as we can go in one day.

Reflection & Prayer

My prayer:
As You search me, Father, take me with You. Reveal to me those areas that I have hidden from myself. Show me, Father, my fears and embarrassments; put a light on those areas that I am not proud of. Let the eyes of my heart be aware of anything that stands between the two of us. Lead me, Father, in the repentance and forgiveness that I need to exercise so that I may imitate You in all things. Amen.

Your Prayer:

_____

_____

_____

_____

_____

_____

_____

_____

_____

_____

_____

_____

_____

Question to Consider:

What fears or anxieties do you have?

_____

_____

_____

_____

_____

_____

_____

_____

_____

_____

_____

_____

_____

_____

_____

_____

_____

Day 7

Change My Heart

The heart is deceitful above all things and beyond cure. Who can understand it?
(Jeremiah 17:9 NIV)

Who indeed? We can rationalize and justify all of our actions. But, who can see the truth of it? Our hearts are full of history and tradition. As we grew, we learned how to respond to different situations. If we were taught as babies not to cry from pain, we may inappropriately laugh as adults. If we witnessed others lying instead of taking responsibility, that is what we mimic. If we were raised with violence, then we ourselves can become violent. We are incapable of changing this behavior or even seeing the wrongness of it without guidance.

One of the most common things that new Christians hear is "You are supposed to be a Christian. You aren't being a good example of it!" What those who don't know Christ (and even some who do) aren't taking into consideration is that we are all works in progress. We will still struggle daily to change old behaviors. Not many of us have the experience of being in the gutter one day and totally transformed the next. But it isn't about that. Our relationship with God is about learning to love Him and allowing Him to show us how to love ourselves and others. It is about recognizing that change is needed. It isn't necessarily an instant change although there are thousands of testimonies that sound like just that. However, so long as we want to change, change is given. God is the only one who sees our whole heart—the broken heart, the twisted heart, the vulnerable heart—and only God can mend it. But He won't without our consent.

Ours is a God of free will. We have the freedom to continue living in pain or the freedom to invite Jesus into our hearts and become that changed person.

Reflection & Prayer

My prayer:
Father, I pray that my heart be tender toward the Holy Spirit and the pain of others. Soften the calluses on my soul so that I may be sensitive again. Be with me today as I begin anew, learning to let go and let You heal my heart. Ease my pain, and teach me how to truly love. Open the eyes of my heart, Father, that I may see others as You see them, not as the world views them. Amen.

Your Prayer:

_____

_____

_____

_____

_____

_____

_____

_____

_____

_____

_____

_____

Question to Consider:

Is there something deceitful in your heart that you haven't given to the Lord to heal?

_____
_____
_____
_____
_____
_____
_____
_____
_____
_____
_____
_____
_____
_____
_____
_____
_____
_____

Week 1 Review

John 3:16
2 Timothy 3:16
1 John 1:9
Genesis 2:15–17; 3:1–5
Hebrews 11:6
Psalm 139:23–24
Jeremiah 17:9

Questions to Consider:

1. *Which verse had the most impact on your life this week? Why?*

_____

_____

2. *Which verse do you think will help you most in the coming week?*

_____

_____

3. *What do these verses tell you about the love of God?*

_____

_____

4. In what ways does your heart deceive you?

_____

_____

5. What did you learn about sin in these verses?

_____

_____

6. What did the Holy Spirit show you about your relationship with God?

_____

_____

7. Review your prayers from this week. How did God speak to you?

_____

_____

8. Did you experience any spiritual growth or resistance? Explain.

_____

_____

_____

_____

_____

_____

Thoughts This Week

The God Who Guides Us

Week 2

Day 1

Soar Like an Eagle

But those who hope in the Lord will renew their strength. They will soar on wings like eagles; they will run and not grow weary, they will walk and not be faint.

(Isaiah 40:31 NIV)

This verse is packed with promise, isn't it? Hope in the Lord is powerful when applied, but the application is the tough part. Let's replace the word hope with some other words of definition. For example, "But those who [trust/believe/desire] the Lord will renew their strength." Substituting synonyms will often bring clarity to the verse. Let's try this with the story of David and Goliath.

When young David fought Goliath, his trust/belief/ desire was in the Lord (1 Samuel 17). Where did he find the hope/belief/trust of sufficient depth to be confident in his challenge? The Israelites had spent forty days trembling at the thought of fighting Goliath. He was a giant whose strength and might were unmatched. And then comes David, a young shepherd, barely a man. He demanded to know why this Goliath would dare to mock the Lord. David stepped up to slay the giant, refusing King Saul's armor and sword. He carefully picked the five stones for his sling. David defeated Goliath because he knew his God was mighty. David didn't just decide he could walk through a cowering army and slay Goliath. He had spent hours among the sheep developing his relationship with God. He knew that God would protect him as he had when David slew lions and bears while guarding the sheep.

With his trust in God, David soared like an eagle. In starting a new project, I am often assailed by doubt. "It is too big." " I am not smart enough." But then I remember this verse (Jeremiah 29:11) and I remember whose daughter I am.

"My Father will walk me through anything. My hope and faith in the Lord is strengthened, and I find confidence. God's plans for me are to prosper, not to harm."

Reflection & Prayer

My prayer:
Father, You are mighty. There is nothing I can't accomplish when my faith is in You. Whatever challenge is before me today, let me put my hope in You. Renew my strength to continue when it seems hopeless. Help me to stand firm and continue to work toward achieving success whether it be in providing for my family, building good working relationships, or overcoming spiritual battles. Thank You, Lord, that I can be confident in You. Amen.

Your Prayer:

_____

_____

_____

_____

_____

_____

_____

_____

_____

Question to Consider:

Is there a challenge in your life that looks like a giant?

_____
_____
_____
_____
_____
_____
_____
_____
_____
_____
_____
_____
_____
_____
_____
_____
_____

Day 2

The Lord Has Prepared a Way

Trust in the Lord with all your heart and lean not on your own understanding.
(Proverbs 3:5 NIV)

Wow! That reminds me of the movie, Indiana Jones and the Last Crusade. There is one scene where Indiana Jones goes through several tests to access the Holy Grail. During his final test, Indiana reaches a cave. But between him and the cave, is a chasm. Here he must take a leap of faith. This is a really deep, heart-stopping chasm! (Talk about leaning not on your own understanding!) Once he takes that step into the chasm, a bridge is revealed. Through an optical illusion, it couldn't be seen from his ledge. He had to trust God because there was no going back.

This is much like our lives and relationship with God. We know that the Lord would never lead us to a place that He hasn't already prepared, but we can't see it. And it looks like a huge leap! At times we have no choice but to trust God. Other times, we have the choice or opportunity to make the decision.

Our chasm might be the unknown of a new place, a new job, leaving an abusive relationship or even a forsaking of what is known and comfortable to start over. Here is our dilemma: Do we accept what our eyes see (or our family says or our past tells us), or do we trust what our hearts know about the love and faithfulness of our Lord? Do we back off from the chasm; or do we step into it, trusting not in our own understanding, but in the plans of the Lord?

Writing this book is my leap of faith. It is a risk unlike any I have ever taken. I have to calm the voices of doubt with every page. But this is where I feel the Lord is leading me. So like Indiana Jones, I will close my eyes and trust that the Lord has prepared the way.

Reflection & Prayer

My prayer:
Father, You have got this even if I don't. I will trust You with all my heart. Help my unbelief, and show me how to have greater faith than I had yesterday. Thank You, Lord, for Your faithfulness. Amen.

Your Prayer:

_____

_____

_____

_____

_____

_____

_____

_____

_____

_____

_____

_____

Question to Consider:

What chasm or challenge are you facing?

Day 3

The Importance of Discipline

"Blessed is the one you discipline, Lord, the one you teach from your law; you grant them relief from days of trouble, till a pit is dug for the wicked. For the Lord will not reject his people; he will never forsake his inheritance. Judgment will again be founded on righteousness, and all the upright in heart will follow it."

(Psalms 94:12–15 NIV)

"Blessed is the one you discipline, Lord." We don't usually think of discipline as a blessing, do we? I didn't. And yet…when is discipline applied? It is applied to correct an action and instill a knowledge of right and wrong. Throughout my life, the only people that I disciplined were those whom I loved. I cared enough to want them to know how to be a valuable member of our society. That comes from contributing in ways that benefit, not harm. As a parent, I didn't apply more discipline than was needed to make the point. And God doesn't either. Of course, it did become harsher the longer it took for the offending action to stop. And God will use even more stringent methods to get our attention if we aren't quick learners.

Conforming to the moral and ethical code of a family builds trust. Whether it is my natural family, my church family, or among business colleagues, I want them to know that I can be trusted to stand by them and to teach them, and guide them in what is right. In this same way, I trust God to teach me. I am a work in progress. Being a mature adult doesn't guarantee that I have all the answers.

I once heard that "An adult produces more than they consume." In fiscal matters, it's true, we produce more than we consume. But what about in other ways? Do you produce more compassion for others than you expect them to provide in return? Have you shown more honesty than you expected from others? How about patience? Have you demonstrated more than others needed to give to you? Think about how much you give grace, patience, and compassion to those around you today.

I want the Lord to discipline me. I want to perform to His standards. I want Him to teach me. This way, I will find relief from anxiety, fear, and repercussions from wrong actions. I will grow in respect and honor. I want to believe that He will not forsake me as one of His heirs.

Reflection & Prayer

My prayer:
Father, I know that Your discipline is never more than is needed. Help me to be aware of Your guidance. Help me to grow in righteousness so that my heart will be pure. Amen.

Your Prayer:

_____

_____

_____

_____

_____

_____

_____

_____

_____

_____

_____

_____

_____

_____

_____

Question to Consider:

How does this change your perception of God?

_____

_____

_____

_____

_____

_____

_____

_____

_____

_____

_____

_____

_____

_____

_____

Day 4

The Lord's Boundaries

"Blessed is the one you discipline, Lord, the one you teach from your law; you grant them relief from days of trouble, till a pit is dug for the wicked. For the Lord will not reject his people; he will never forsake his inheritance. Judgment will again be founded on righteousness, and all the upright in heart will follow it."

(Psalms 94:12–15 NIV)

As I was thinking about those I love I considered those who love or care about me in return. My parents, of course, disciplined me. They grew up in the early part of the 1900s. Their discipline was swift and, at times, harsh. But when I compare it to what they were used to growing up, they were gentler.

Their generation was slowly turning more attention to the raising of people, not just children. And I tried to be a better parent than they were. I am not sure if I did any better than my own parents, but I certainly didn't do any worse.

Setting boundaries creates security. There is a comfort in knowing that someone is watching over us. It gives us a sense of safety.

Just as we set boundaries for toddlers, so do teenagers need and want boundaries. As a teenager, I remember using my parents as an excuse not to do something. A friend might ask me to accompany them somewhere; and if I was uneasy about it, I would say, "Oh, shoot! My mom won't let me. She is so awful sometimes!" There were times my mom knew nothing about it, but I was comfortable relying on her. Since the other kids knew my parents were strict, they didn't push me any further. I felt safe. Hence their boundaries for me gave me a safety net when I was placed in an uncomfortable position. It later allowed me to set boundaries for myself as an adult.

Parents aren't the only ones who discipline. Employers, supervisors, and managers all need to correct behavior at one time or another. I have worked with some who were very good at it. They cared about the growth of their employees. They wanted to help me grow past my current position. They saw potential and encouraged development. I had one manager who was a lovely person but had decided ahead of time that I wasn't as good as my previous manager told them I was.

We didn't know each other well; but in business, as in life, preconceived notions take hold and it is difficult to move past them. This manager didn't care enough to discipline or correct me. She had very little interaction with me, so I was left to wonder how I should be doing my job better. It was a stressful and helpless situation to be in.

Luckily, God does care. He wants us to continue to develop in our relationship with Him. He wants us to feel secure and safe. He wants us to live within the boundaries He set. Knowing that there are rules is comforting.

Reflection & Prayer

My prayer:
Father, thank You for loving me enough to set boundaries.
Thank You for showing me how to remain safe. I appreciate
knowing what is expected. I can live calmly in the knowledge
that You will always show me the way. Amen.

Your Prayer:

_____

_____

_____

_____

_____

_____

_____

_____

_____

_____

_____

_____

_____

Question to Consider:

How does this change your perception of God and what He wants for you?

Day 5

Thank You For Creation

"For my thoughts are not your thoughts, neither are your ways my ways," declares the Lord. "As the heavens are higher than the earth, so are my ways higher than your ways and my thoughts than your thoughts."

(Isaiah 55:8, 9 NIV)

It is good once in a while to be reminded of the largeness of God. I get so comfortable talking with Him that I tend to shrink Him down to the size of one of my friends. I need to witness the magnitude of Him, to see the world from His eyes. I love the Sesame Street song that goes, "Where you put your eyes, that's about the size, that's about the size of it."

Imagine the wonder that astronauts are able to experience while orbiting the Earth or standing on the moon. To be able to glimpse all of God's creation all at once must be exhilarating!

And yet, God also sees every sparrow in the sky and every hair on my head. How can He see the microscopic at the same time that He is aware of the mountains and oceans, the sky over our heads, and the vastness of the cosmos? Who is this wondrous being that He should care about us? Who loves us so much that He gave his only begotten Son that we might have life everlasting?

Think of His generosity toward us. We can go to Him with all our problems and never be turned away. We can go to Him with our sorrows and be comforted. He rejoices with us. No emotion that we have is new. No temptation is so great that He won't provide a way for us to stand up under it.

Reflection & Prayer

My prayer:
Thank You, Lord, that You not only take notice of me but truly love me. Your creation is beyond comprehension. I worship You, Lord. Amen.

Your Prayer:

_____

_____

_____

_____

_____

_____

_____

_____

_____

_____

_____

_____

Question to Consider:

What does this verse tell you about God?

_____
_____
_____
_____
_____
_____
_____
_____
_____
_____
_____
_____
_____
_____
_____
_____

Day 6

Power of Prayer

Whoever of you loves life and desires to see many good days, Keep your tongue from evil and your lips from telling lies. Turn from evil and do good; seek peace and pursue it.

(Psalms 34:12–14 NIV)

In our daily life, we tend to forget that Jesus is right there beside us, witnessing every action, thought, and word. It is so easy to snap at a child, spouse, friend, or co-worker when they come to us while we're trying to concentrate on something else. In my own life, I've been short with a coworker who was trying to give me information while I was on the phone. The information may relate to the client I was speaking with, but my impatience showed. There are many instances in my life that I wish I could go back and apologize for my words. Seeing them through the eyes of a woman, not the eyes of a teenager or child, I have the distance to recognize how hurtful it must have been to be on the receiving end of my frustration.

We can't go back, but we can ask the Holy Spirit to calm and heal the hurt of the other person. Our daily struggle to be our best is constant. The Lord didn't ask for perfection when he died on the cross for us. He only asked for a commitment to strive to be better, to love Him, and to love one another. Don't be discouraged if you have to ask for the same assistance daily. You aren't alone. It does not matter how perfect the lady in the seventh pew appears to be. She has her own struggles with pain, anger, jealousy, and so on.

In 2 Corinthians 12:7–9, Paul says that he pled with the Lord to take the thorn from his side, but that the Lord said, "My grace is sufficient for you." Even Paul the Apostle had daily struggles with the same issue.

Our prayers don't only reveal something about ourselves, but our perspective of those around us as well. In the development of my relationship with God, He has shown me how to pray for others.

There was a time I admired our pastor's wife and wished to be more like her. I prayed that the Lord would show me how to accomplish this. What the Holy Spirit showed me was a heart of spun glass, fine and brittle, so delicate it could break at the least bit of pressure. It opened my eyes to the life of a minister's wife—under constant scrutiny, afraid to make the slightest misstep for fear of how it would reflect on her husband. That was not what I wanted. I began to pray for an easing of her tension, that she be surrounded by godly women who could be trusted not to gossip about her or judge her or her family for being human.

I prayed that my words be sincere and true. False flattery

is a form of lying. If I can't be genuine in my speech, then I try to refrain from commenting. I learned early on that instead of giving compliments that I didn't mean, I would offer ones that I did mean. I may not find a friend's dress style flattering, but I could honestly say the color brought out the sparkle in her eyes. It was uplifting for both of us.

Reflection & Prayer

My prayer:
Lord, I do love the life You have given me. I am truly blessed and look forward to being closer to You because words can wound for a lifetime. Help me to turn from that which saddens You. Help me to remember that anything that harms another, however unintentionally, is a sin. Guide me in understanding and repentance so that I may receive forgiveness. Only then will my heart be clean and carefree and full of Your peace. Amen.

Your Prayer:

_____

_____

_____

_____

_____

_____

_____

_____

_____

Question to Consider:

Where does this verse lead you today?

_____

_____

_____

_____

_____

_____

_____

_____

_____

_____

_____

_____

_____

_____

_____

_____

_____

_____

Day 7

Bearing Witness

You shall not give false testimony against your neighbor.
(Exodus 20:16 NIV)

I have caught myself getting ready to repeat neighborhood "news" when I stopped to think, "How do I know this is true?" It may not be malicious in intent, but I like to think about these questions before opening my mouth to speak on another: Was it heard through my perception of that person? Did I witness the action with eyes of truth? It is often impossible to know, isn't it?

Police know how unreliable eyewitness testimony is because they often get different information about an incident from multiple people. It's important to understand that our history will cloud our clarity. Our preconceived ideas about a person will add a depth or layer to the information that isn't actually there.

Say, I see Janette, whom I don't know well, emptying Carol's garbage into a box. I may speculate and think Janette is being nosy. Telling Chuck about the action can set off a whole wildfire of gossip about Janette, who as it turns out, accidentally threw away her retainer while at Carol's for dinner. Ah, the danger of offhanded remarks and speculation!

Bearing false witness is often like the old game of telephone. With each telling, something is added whether through an urge to embellish or simply because the hearer was only half listening. We want to share with others. We love to talk! We want to commiserate and celebrate and be angry or hopeful for our friends. What we don't want is to add elements that aren't there.

For some, like me, the whole story including the details is enthralling. I want to know how someone felt or reacted and why. I just need to beware not to speculate about it.

Reflection & Prayer

My prayer:
Dear Lord, help me to remember that Your love for all means
that I am to filter everything I say through Your eyes of truth. I
am weak in some areas and need Your restraint. Amen.

Your Prayer:

_____

_____

_____

_____

_____

_____

_____

_____

_____

_____

_____

_____

_____

Question to Consider:

What is God telling you through this verse?

_____
_____
_____
_____
_____
_____
_____
_____
_____
_____
_____
_____
_____
_____
_____
_____

Week 2 Review

Isaiah 40:31
Proverbs 3:5
Psalm 94:12–15
Isaiah 55:8–9
Psalm 34:12–14
Exodus 20:16

Questions to Consider:

1. Which verse had the greatest impact on you this week?

_____

_____

2. This week you learned about the discipline of God. How does this change your perception of God?

_____

_____

3. Why do you think that we are told to guard our tongues?

_____

_____

Glenda Keiper

4. Which verses gave you the most hope this week?

_____

_____

5. What impact will these verses have in the week ahead?

_____

_____

6. Review your prayers from this week. How did God speak to you this week?

_____

_____

_____

_____

_____

_____

_____

_____

_____

_____

_____

_____

_____

Thoughts This Week

_____
_____
_____
_____
_____
_____
_____
_____
_____
_____
_____
_____
_____
_____
_____
_____
_____
_____
_____
_____
_____
_____

Jesus Our Savior

Week 3

Day 1

The "Simple" Carpenter

In the beginning was the Word, and the Word was with God and
the Word was God. He was with God in the beginning. Through
him all things were made; without him nothing was made that has
been made.

(John 1:1–3 NIV)

Recently, I learned that the way I had been thinking of
Jesus had a serious flaw. I had learned that he was a "simple
carpenter." Jesus, the man, is described as tuetōn: an
architect, craftsman, or builder. Although carpenters possess
great skill, there were very few trees in Nazareth—only fig
and olive, which aren't good for building. It is much more
likely that he worked with stone as well as wood. No wonder
so many of his references were to stone.

He was with God at the beginning of creation. He was

an architect of creation! Jesus is not "simple" at all. He has an intimate knowledge of so much more than geometric concepts, the properties of stone, and the importance of foundations. Through Jesus, the Heavens and the Earth were created. He is the Creator of our weather, our seasons, and overall the self-contained terrarium we call Earth. How extraordinary that he was able to communicate with us of limited intelligence! What love he must have for us! When I try to think of the scope, the sheer size of the works of his hands, my brain begins to hurt. I don't have the capacity for it. Add to that the knowledge that a Crucifixion and Resurrection would be needed for our salvation! I am so humbled that his love for us includes so much intention.

Let's talk about the Resurrection. All the major religions have prophets, but Christianity is the only one that has a resurrection. Our Savior, as the architect of our salvation, was more than just a prophet. His physical death was temporary. He rose from the dead to offer us life everlasting. Talk about intentional actions! His crucifixion wasn't the end of the story, but neither was his resurrection. His story began with a virgin birth and continued through his ministry, crucifixion, and resurrection. And though it was foretold hundreds of years before his birth, the Almighty architect's story didn't end with an empty tomb. Here it is two thousand years later, and God is still using this timeless event to save those who believe in Christ and his sacrifice.

Reflection & Prayer

My prayer:
Father, thank You that You purposefully and with full intention created not only our world but everything in it. Thank You for creating us, loving us with such fullness that You provided a sacrifice that I may be able to come before You; it is almost more than I can understand. Thank You for the wind, the seasons, the cycle of birth, and life and death. Thank You that all plants regenerate and are there for our use. Thank You for knowing not only how it all began, but how it will all end. Guide me today so that I may walk with intention, aware of every action and its consequence. Amen.

Your Prayer:

_____

_____

_____

_____

_____

_____

_____

_____

_____

Question to Consider:

What image do you have of Jesus?

_____
_____
_____
_____
_____
_____
_____
_____
_____
_____
_____
_____
_____
_____
_____
_____
_____

Day 2

The Presence of Christ

They went to Capernaum, and when the Sabbath came, Jesus went in the synagogue and began to teach. The people were amazed at his teaching, because he taught them as one who had authority, not as the teachers of the law.

(Mark 1:21, 22 NIV)

During the time of Jesus, a man couldn't become a rabbi until he was thirty years old. He gained experience by traveling to villages and gathering people to listen to him. This way, he also gained maturity and an understanding of life.

There is something called the "rule of know". This states that once you learn something, you can't remember what it was like to not know it. That's why I believe that once they had a congregation most rabbis forgot what it was like not knowing how to read.

They used imagery to explain the Torah. However, their world was one of the written word in an alpha-numeric language. Every letter was represented by a number and vice versa. A language rich in symbols and deeper meanings, depending on how the letters were combined.

It makes me wonder, in their excitement over these words, were they able to relate to the uneducated people in the countryside? They could recite the words as a scribe would, but could they convey the emotion held within them?

Few, if any, in the village could read. All of their knowledge, ancestry, and history had been passed down orally. Into this arena comes a young man, a rabbi, who not only speaks with authority but relates knowledge in a way that they can understand. He uses the imagery of animals, buildings, flowers, and millstones; all things the everyday person could understand and relate to. He was a carpenter and builder by trade. He was raised in the region and knew the ways of the people.

He commanded their attention and spoke to their hearts. He spoke of love, of the Father, and of a Heavenly kingdom. He spoke of forgiveness freely given. How powerful it must have been to sit at his feet and learn. How powerful his spiritual presence must have been! I imagine that each person felt as if he were speaking only with them. A presence so overwhelming yet humble, that some turned away. But for those who didn't turn away, they must have felt his love! Being that close to Jesus, how could one not relax and rejoice in his presence?

Reflection & Prayer

My prayer:
Father, today let me sit at Your feet. Fill me not just with the words of the Bible, but with the emotion of the words. Let me feel the joy and peace radiate from them. Give me the wisdom to use what I know in a way that others can relate to, in a way that will expand their knowledge of Your glory. Let my words be a beacon to others of Your goodness and love.
Amen.

Your Prayer:

_____

_____

_____

_____

_____

_____

_____

_____

_____

_____

_____

_____

Question to Consider:

In what way do you learn best (hearing, reading, discussing, etc.)? Why is it important to meet with others?

_____

_____

_____

_____

_____

_____

_____

_____

_____

_____

_____

_____

_____

_____

Day 3

The Sin Not Stated in the Bible

Then Jesus said to his disciples, "Whoever wants to be my disciple must deny themselves and take up their cross and follow me. For whoever wants to save their life will lose it, but whoever loses their life for me will find it."

(Matthew 16:24–25)

I once heard a pastor say, "Smoking isn't going to send you to hell, but it will make you smell as if you have already been there." It was good for a chuckle, but as I thought about it, God impressed upon my heart that my cigarettes were causing me to put my time with loved ones aside for that addiction. My children had to wait for help so I could finish my cigarette. Our errands were delayed so I could have one last puff. It was my form of gluttony. So I quit. I received prayer and the Holy Spirit removed the desire

Anything that stands between us and God is sinful whether it is easily identified, such as murder or theft, or more insidious, like sloth or gluttony. Whatever we do in excess and/or to the exclusion of other people or things must be put aside.

Another insidious little sin is giving a full backstory when asking for prayer. How could filling in details be a sin? Does your backstory contain gossip about yourself or others? Think about that. I realized that the details that I was giving to help others pray for me were actually being used to make the other person look bad. It was a way of building myself up by tearing someone else down. God doesn't need the details, and neither does anyone else. The Holy Spirit will prompt us on how to pray. And while I may want God to move a coworker away from me, He may be leading someone to pray for the pain in that person's life, an easing of their burdens. Another will be prompted to pray for peace to reign in our workplace. And yet another may pray for the eyes of my heart to be opened to my actions and how they contributed to the situation.

We are sinful by nature. We need to have a heightened awareness of denying ourselves and following Jesus. I lost the old me in so many ways to follow Jesus. But it is a daily struggle. There is always a new obstacle to overcome to take up my cross and follow him.

Reflection & Prayer

My prayer:
Father, help me to be sensitive to ways wherein I may be indulging myself. I want to drop my pride and walk in humility with You. I need assistance in giving up (today's issue) and growing in Your Word. Holy Spirit, enlighten me. Give me wisdom and strength. Show me how to find joy and peace, extending kindness to friends and strangers alike. Amen.

Your Prayer:

_____

_____

_____

_____

_____

_____

_____

_____

_____

_____

Question to Consider:

What is one thing that comes between you and a fuller relationship with Jesus? Are you willing to put it aside?

_____

_____

_____

_____

_____

_____

_____

_____

_____

_____

_____

_____

_____

_____

_____

_____

_____

Day 4

Renewed Relationship with God

"One of the teachers of the law came and heard them debating. Noticing that Jesus had given them a good answer, he asked him, "Of all the commandments, which is the most important?"

"The most important one," answered Jesus, "is this: 'Hear, O Israel: The Lord our God, the Lord is one. Love the Lord your God with all your heart and with all your soul and with all your mind and with all your strength.'

(Mark 12:28-30 NIV)

Jesus, though he was the Son of God, always put God the Father in the highest position. His mission here on Earth was to bring people into a closer relationship with God, to mend the brokenness caused by Adam. Throughout the Old Testament, the Jews fought and rejected God. Time and again, He brought them into a place of safety, gathering up the remnants when they were almost completely wiped out. He ensured that they were brought in and out of captivity and sent prophets to warn them about straying too far from Him.

Jesus was the means for them, and now for us, to attain a renewed relationship with God. Though at the time, many Jews rejected him as the Messiah, many others followed him. "Love the Lord your God with all your heart, and with all your soul, and with all your mind, and with all your strength."

Though sometimes the terms heart and soul are interchangeable, the heart is where the emotions reside, and the soul is where the life force resides. Our mind makes decisions, and our strength is our physical body. We are to place God first in our emotions, our life, our decisions, and our bodies— to love God with all of our beings. In our daily lives, it is this dedication that we are to use to filter all our actions, from what we read to what we eat.

I struggle with the completeness of this sometimes. I'm sure I'm not alone. When I am careful about the type of books I read or television programs I watch, I am much more relaxed. My emotions are not easily riled by the actions of others. I am more apt to extend grace to others when they make mistakes or are rude. My decisions are more balanced. It is easy to feel the immediate reaction when our bodies have too much food and drink. Each of these parts are connected to the others just as the bones of our body are connected by muscle and tendon. God made us this way. I think in wonder of the completeness of his creation. He should be first in my heart, soul, mind, and body.

Reflection & Prayer

My prayer:
Father, everything that You created is connected. Just as the evaporation and condensation of water are part of the life cycle of the planet, so too are we made of more than one component that is interconnected. Thank You for caring about all of me today and always. Amen.

Your Prayer:

_____

_____

_____

_____

_____

_____

_____

_____

_____

_____

_____

_____

Question to Consider:

What does this say about your relationship with God?

_____
_____
_____
_____
_____
_____
_____
_____
_____
_____
_____
_____
_____
_____
_____
_____
_____

Day 5

Love Others Fully

The second is this: "Love your neighbor as yourself. There is no commandment greater than these."
(Mark 12:31 NIV)

We are to love our neighbors in the same way that we love ourselves. Do you love yourself; really love yourself? I struggle with this at times because there is nothing like a small town to let you know just how imperfect your life is. It took years for me to understand that God forgot my past when he forgave my sins—that I was a new creation.

In order to love our neighbor, we must be able to love ourselves first. To truly love ourselves, we must recognize that God loves us and created us as we are for a specific purpose. Until we can love ourselves, we cannot truly love others. We will always be aware of the shortcomings that

93

we see in ourselves. Only once we can love ourselves fully, can we see others through the eyes of God. Self-love allows us to recognize the hurt in others. We can put their needs first because there is no fear—no fear that the money we spend will be needed later, no fear that we will be made fun of or rejected for offering to help, no fear that people will take advantage of us.

The struggles we have prepare us to witness to others and minister to them in a way that those not acquainted with struggle can't. Those that were once gang members can relate to those that are currently in gangs. Those raised in poverty have an intimate knowledge of what others in poverty are going through. Those who were felons and have found forgiveness are the best to minister to those in prison. Alcoholics understand the daily fight that other alcoholics have. God knows our sins, our struggles, and our past. There is no circumstance that He can't use.

No matter what you think of yourself, God values you. He loves the person you were, are, and are trying to be. Once you can accept that, you will be able to love others with fullness. Look at yourself through the eyes of God, and soon you will see others through His eyes.

Reflection & Prayer

My prayer:
Lord, thank You for loving me when I cannot love myself. Let me always see myself and others with Your eyes, looking for the good. Help me to value myself as one of Your children.
Amen.

Your Prayer:

_____

_____

_____

_____

_____

_____

_____

_____

_____

_____

_____

_____

_____

Question to Consider:

What do you struggle with that you think God sees with a better sight than you do?

_____
_____
_____
_____
_____
_____
_____
_____
_____
_____
_____
_____
_____
_____

Day 6

Your Sole Job

*The second is this: "Love your neighbor as yourself. There is no
commandment greater than these."*
(Mark 12:31 NIV)

Love your neighbor. It is an all-encompassing phrase, not
just restricted to those that are in your neighborhood. Love
others as you love yourself. Love mankind—all of mankind.
This includes those you don't like. This includes those of
differing ethnic or cultural backgrounds. This includes those
who are of a different sexual orientation than you and those
whose political views oppose yours.

So many have not only been rejected by Christians but
really devastated, to the point that all Christians are hateful
in their eyes. How do we change this perception? By loving
our neighbor. By saying, "I see you. I hear your hurt. I may

97

not agree with you, but I am willing to have a discussion. What can I do to ease your pain?"

God doesn't call upon us to like or agree with everything and everyone, but we are called upon to love them. Respect their differences, and accept their differences. Love them and see to their needs. We are not called upon to "fix" them. Our job is to love them and share the good news of Jesus. If they reject that, we are to still love them. Jesus knew humans in a variety of colors and social situations, and not one was loved more than another. His followers came because of his love, not his condemnation. There were a variety of sinners, and he accepted them all. We are all on a level playing field in his eyes. And we show our love for him through the way we show love to others.

We are called upon to be shining examples of love in a hopeless world. We are called upon to have compassion and listen to their pain. God is the final judge. He will have the conversations with them about their lives, not us. Our job is to shine as an example of God's love. To do this, we need to first see others through God's eyes. "He so loved the world, [the entire world], that he gave His only begotten Son that we have life everlasting."

I have been shown ways lately that I have hurt others unintentionally. Not by calling them out, but by not recognizing and validating their hurt even when they don't recognize my own hurt. That's a tough call. "You hurt me and refuse to recognize it, so why should I care about your feelings?" We care because God said to love my neighbor as myself.

On social media, it is common for an opinion to be posted with the author wanting no conversation other than agreement. I had to stop trying to have conversations because it was causing more dissension than conversation. There are so many hurting people in our world. What we can do is love, accept and validate their feelings. We can be the one who cares without condemnation. Be the one who brings meals or offers rides. Be the one who stands in the gap. Be the action of the Christian faith. Feel this empowering knowledge that your sole job is to love and be a beacon of that love to bring others close to God.

Reflection & Prayer

My prayer:
Father, open the eyes of my heart. Show me ways that I can
love others. Teach me how to love them as You love me.
Amen.

Your Prayer:

_____

_____

_____

_____

_____

_____

_____

_____

_____

_____

_____

_____

Question to Consider:

What does this verse reveal to you about God's love?

_____

_____

_____

_____

_____

_____

_____

_____

_____

_____

_____

_____

_____

_____

_____

_____

Day 7

No Action Goes Unnoticed

Some women were watching from a distance. Among them were Mary Magdalene, Mary the mother of James the younger and of Joseph, and Salome. In Galilee, these women had followed him and cared for his needs. Many other women who had come up with him to Jerusalem were also there.

(Mark 15:40–41 NIV)

This verse takes place at the crucifixion. When I first read this verse, I was struck by the strength of these women. It must have been incredibly painful to watch the torture and death of the man that they had followed and tended to. Unlike the men, the women had an intimate relationship with Jesus. Not a sexual relationship, but one of anticipating his needs and caring for him on a personal level. The men haven't cooked for him or washed his clothes. They haven't prepared water for his washing or seen to his comfort. The

Bible mentions the men being with him while he is teaching, but this verse says that these women had followed him from Galilee. They were with him as silent witnesses. These women witnessed his weariness and responded to it.

Think of how you respond to those you love. You know when your children need to eat or sleep. You know when a parent you may be caring for needs assistance. You know when the person you love needs someone to listen to them as they vent about the frustrations of the day. This was the relationship between Jesus and these women who witnessed his final moments on the cross.

Have you ever noticed that when God mentions women, it is because something of significance is happening? It seems that way to me. Women like Mary and Elizabeth, Sarah and Hagar, Rahab, Ruth, Esther, and Hannah, were integral parts of important events.

I believe that God wanted this verse included to ensure that we knew that no action goes unnoticed. There is no action so insignificant that he doesn't see it. Every action you perform for someone, no matter how unappreciated you feel, is noticed by God. He sees the care you take, whether offering a stranger a kind word or preparing lunch. You may not think it is worth mentioning, but God does. He made sure that the world knew about the behind-the-scenes actions of these devoted women. God, too, is with us constantly. He does things for us that we don't notice. He knows when we are exhausted and when we need a little boost.

I love looking for ways that God shows He loves me in the seemingly insignificant events in my life, those "lucky" moments. When I am in a hurry and another cashier opens for me, or when I am feeling down and I get a note in the mail for no reason. These are little love notes from God, saying, "I see you and love you."

Reflection & Prayer

My prayer:
Father, thank You that You see everything. I may feel underappreciated at times by those around me, but You know the effort I have put into caring for others. Help me to remember that You give me the same love and care. When I don't notice, remind me that Your hand is still at work in my life. Thank You for the love You have for me. Amen.

Your Prayer:

_____

_____

_____

_____

_____

_____

_____

_____

_____

_____

_____

Question to Consider:

How does this change your perception of God's love?

_____

_____

_____

_____

_____

_____

_____

_____

_____

_____

_____

_____

_____

_____

_____

_____

Week 3 Review

John 1:1–3
Mark 1:21–22
Matthew 16:24–25
Mark 12:28–30
Mark 12:31
Mark 15:40–41

Questions to Consider:

1. *Which verse had the greatest impact on you this week?*

_____

_____

2. *What do these verses tell you about Jesus?*

_____

_____

3. *How can you show your love for Jesus?*

_____

_____

4. Why do you think that Jesus highlighted the two greatest commandments?

_____

_____

5. What did you learn this week about God's love for you?

_____

_____

6. How will these verses help you in the coming week?

_____

_____

7. Review your prayers from this week. How did God speak to you this week?

_____

_____

_____

_____

_____

_____

_____

_____

_____

Thoughts This Week

_____
_____
_____
_____
_____
_____
_____
_____
_____
_____
_____
_____
_____
_____
_____
_____
_____
_____
_____

Jesus
Our Teacher

Week 4

There Are No Accidents

"And a woman was there who had been subject to bleeding for twelve years, but no one could heal her. She came up behind him and touched the edge of his cloak, and immediately her bleeding stopped.

"Who touched me?" Jesus asked. When they all denied it, Peter said, "Master, the people are crowding and pressing against you." But Jesus said, "Someone touched me; I know that power has gone out from me."

Then the woman, seeing that she could not go unnoticed, came trembling and fell at his feet. In the presence of all the people, she told why she had touched him and how she had been instantly healed. Then he said to her, "Daughter, your faith has healed you. Go in peace."

(Luke 8:43-48 NIV)

Jesus knew immediately that he had been touched. I have never thought about his power being so present and physical that it emanated from him. This was an "Aha!" moment for me. His intentional actions are recorded, but I wonder how many healings were done unintentionally just because someone with faith was close enough to rub up against his cloak. But there is nothing unintentional about God and His plan.

His creation, the prophecies in the Old Testament about the coming of His Son, everything has been with intention. God has no accidents in His plan.

Jesus was aware of the power flowing from him. He called the woman out and used her faith as an example of the power and love of God. He wasn't angry that an unclean person had touched him. He changed the rules that the Jewish community was living by. He was more concerned with the woman and her inner being than he was about how her touch might affect his standing in the community. He was impressed with her faith. He blessed her, telling her to "Go in peace".

When I renewed my commitment to Christ as an adult, I was fully aware of my sins, and my uncleanliness. I knew that I didn't deserve to ask for forgiveness and acceptance from God. But like this woman, I wanted to be cleaned. I trusted that the God who gave His only Son as a sacrifice for our sins would extend grace and mercy to me.

No, there are no accidents in His plan. He knew every one of us before we were whispers in the wind. He knew our lives, and He knew that He would love us enough to extend salvation to each.

Reflection & Prayer

My prayer:
Father, daily I learn more from Your Word about You, Jesus,
and the Holy Spirit. Daily I learn more about Your intentions
and plans for my life. Thank You, Father, for Your grace and
mercy that allows me to draw close to You. Thank You for
cleansing me of sin and blessing me. Amen.

Your Prayer:

_____

_____

_____

_____

_____

_____

_____

_____

_____

_____

_____

Question to Consider:

How does Jesus's response reflect God's grace?

_____

_____

_____

_____

_____

_____

_____

_____

_____

_____

_____

_____

_____

_____

_____

_____

_____

_____

Faith Builds and Delivers

"And a woman was there who had been subject to bleeding for twelve years, but no one could heal her. She came up behind him and touched the edge of his cloak, and immediately her bleeding stopped.

"Who touched me?" Jesus asked. When they all denied it, Peter said, "Master, the people are crowding and pressing against you." But Jesus said, "Someone touched me; I know that power has gone out from me."

Then the woman, seeing that she could not go unnoticed, came trembling and fell at his feet. In the presence of all the people, she told why she had touched him and how she had been instantly healed. Then he said to her, "Daughter, your faith has healed you. Go in peace."

(Luke 8:43-48 NIV)

That the woman was able to walk at all is a miracle in my mind. Having had an issue of bleeding for that long, it is amazing that her red blood cells could recover fast enough to keep her alive. Never mind walking!

I suffered for several months from anemia so severe that I would fall because there weren't enough red blood cells to supply my muscles with what they needed to function. How desperate she must have been to leave her house and put forth the physical effort, join the crowd, just to get close enough to touch his cloak. It must have been so exhausting to fight her way through to him.

In Jewish law, feminine bleeding was unclean; and if an unclean person touched another, they also became unclean. Women who were bleeding were supposed to separate themselves. She took a huge risk in coming out into a crowd. She risked making Jesus unclean. But in her desperation, she also found faith so strong that she was sure this man could heal her. He had healed others and driven out demons. Surely, he would not deny her. Surely, he would take pity on her and heal her of this crippling condition.

So she grabbed the hem of his cloak, whether to get his attention or because it was as close as she could get with the last of her energy. Then power flowed from him into her, healing her immediately. She must have experienced such elation! To finally feel whole and have the ability to walk without tiring.

Once discovered, she came fearfully before him. But Jesus didn't ridicule or react in anger. He commended her on her faith and pronounced her healed. Jesus not only healed her—his touch cleansed her. Not only did he bless her, but he called her "daughter." How all-encompassing is his love? He claimed her as family. To hear those words after all she had been through! She would no longer have to separate herself from others. She could once again join society; join the company of others.

What can we learn from this faithful woman? Faith builds and delivers. Expect great things, and great things happen. Our faith frees us in so many ways. It heals us from wounds, seen and unseen. It cleanses us and releases us. Faith's power can be truly transformative, as this woman learned.

Reflection & Prayer

My prayer:
Father, increase my faith. I want to be in a place where I can confidently expect miracles. I want to trust You as much as this woman. Increase my faith, Lord, that others may see Your greatness. Amen.

Your Prayer:

_____

_____

_____

_____

_____

_____

_____

_____

_____

_____

_____

_____

Question to Consider:

How does the faith of the woman in the passage help you to understand how God views your faith?

_____

_____

_____

_____

_____

_____

_____

_____

_____

_____

_____

_____

_____

_____

_____

_____

Day 3

We Must Forgive

*Be kind and compassionate to one another, forgiving each other,
just as in Christ God forgave you.*
(Ephesians 4:32 NIV)

"Forgiving each other, just as in Christ, God forgave
you." How exactly did Christ forgive us? His forgiveness is
wholeheartedly and without reservation. When we accept
Christ, our sins are forgiven freely. There are no strings
or further actions needed. He forgave and forgot. His
forgiveness was freely given.

Forgiveness is sometimes difficult to accept. We may
think we don't deserve it or don't need it. We can justify
any action or words. I think forgiving ourselves is just
as important as forgiving others. To truly accept God's
forgiveness, we must accept our sinfulness. And once

forgiven, we must forget.

As I speak with other Christians, unforgiveness is the biggest stumbling block in their walk. And while they may be aware that they are not able to forgive, they don't see it as a sin that ripples out into other interactions. They are so angry with a teacher or a pastor that they don't really want to give up that hurt. Even harder is forgiving a spouse or family member for the pain they caused, be it emotional or physical. That anger and pain becomes something so large that it attaches itself to us and weighs us down physically, emotionally, and most importantly spiritually. In this space of unforgiveness, you may not even see the millstone around your neck, affecting all your other decisions.

We can come up with all kinds of reasons to not forgive someone. They didn't apologize or admit they were wrong. They don't care that they hurt me, so why should I forgive them? My pain is too big. They don't deserve to be forgiven... Or they did apologize, but it wasn't enough. My hurt will never be assuaged. They hurt me for years. Am I just supposed to forgive them and forget that? Yes.*

"Be kind and compassionate to one another, forgiving each other, just as in Christ God forgave you." Our unwillingness to forgive stands between us and a loving God, keeping us from enjoying a full relationship with Him. There is nothing we can't do when we ask the Holy Spirit for assistance. For with Christ, all things are possible.

*Though we are supposed to forgive, we are not called on to stay in abusive situations. God did not intend for women or men to turn the other cheek to being mentally or physically abused. If you find yourself advised by people, whether a pastor or family members, that use God's word to encourage you to stay in an abusive situation, please find a way to remove yourself from them. The Bible uses the term "oppression" instead of abuse. Oppression means prolonged cruel or unjust treatment or control, mental pressure, or distress. Any form of oppression or violence is "detestable to the Lord" (Isaiah 49:26).

For more information on the biblical view of domestic violence please scan the QR codes below or type in the links located at the bottom of the page.

| The Bible On... | Emotional Abuse in the Local Church | What Does the Bible Say About Destructive and Abusive Relationships? |

https://www.saferresource.org.au/the_bible_on_domestic_family_violence

https://www.focusonthefamily.com/get-help/emotional-abuse-in-the-local-church/

https://marriagemissions.com/bible-destructive-abusive-relationships/

Reflection & Prayer

My prayer:
Father, in my own strength, I can't forgive and forget. The damage to my inner self is so big. It hurts so much. By myself, I just can't let go of it. Holy Spirit, I need You to help me. Fill the hole that letting go will leave with Your peace and love. Help me to say the words, "I forgive you" until I feel it truly in my heart. It is big, Father—perhaps the biggest thing You have ever asked of me—but I know I can do it if You will walk me through it. Thank You for the forgiveness You freely offered me. Amen.

Your Prayer:

_____

_____

_____

_____

_____

_____

_____

_____

_____

_____

Question to Consider:

Is there someone that you need to forgive, regardless of whether they have asked for forgiveness or not?

Acts of Love

Do not repay evil with evil or insult with insult. On the contrary,
repay evil with blessing, because to this you were called so that you
may inherit a blessing.

(1 Peter 3:9 NIV)

How could God even ask this of us? Repay evil with a
blessing? How does that work? The Old Testament told us
"an eye for an eye". When did that rule change? It changed
when Jesus came and sacrificed his life for us. In the Old
Testament, there was no intermediary to go between God
and us. Justice was meted out here on Earth, and a sacrifice
was offered to atone for sins.

Jesus came to atone for our sins. Every single one of
them was wiped clean the moment we accepted him as Lord
and Savior. We are to stand as examples of his love. Grace
was freely extended to us, and we are to extend grace to

others. I know! It is a lot to ask.

When we are wronged, our hearts rebel. "But," you might say, "that person stole from me or embarrassed me or wounded me. My heart will never be whole again!"

When we seek revenge, it stirs up a hornet's nest of other emotions: anger, resentment, jealousy, unforgiveness, and mistrust. Every one of these stands between us and a loving God. How can we, who have been forgiven everything, hold someone else to a higher account?

Refusing to allow others to dictate our reactions is a process of growth. The faith that we show when we extend a blessing to one who has harmed us, enriches our relationship with God.

Corrie Ten Boom in her book, The Hiding Place, speaks of being asked to forgive a man who was a cruel guard at the concentration camp where she was kept as a prisoner. He had become a Christian since the war and was asking forgiveness. She knew in her heart that it was what God wanted, but how could she? Her anger and hurt said, "No!" But she asked the Holy Spirit to help her. She and the man met there in forgiveness as she was led by the Holy Spirit.

Consider how your reaction affects others. It ripples outward, either repelling or drawing others in. It will stand as a beacon of God's love or represent a God intent on inflicting pain. When someone who doesn't believe in Christ sees you repay evil with evil, they feel justified in their unbelief. But, when a blessing repays evil, it causes confusion and curiosity. They wonder where you get the strength to control your anger and act in love.

Reflection & Prayer

My prayer:
Father, this wrong committed against me hurts. I am filled with anger and I want to hurt them back. Open the eyes of my heart, Lord, that I may understand the pain the other person is dealing with, the fear that controls their life, the anger that consumes them. Give me the grace, Holy Spirit, to respond in kindness. Let me respond not as one whose actions are controlled by others, but as one whose actions bring glory to You. Amen.

Your Prayer:

_____

_____

_____

_____

_____

_____

_____

_____

_____

_____

Question to Consider:

In what ways can you allow God to change your heart when you are wronged?

_____

_____

_____

_____

_____

_____

_____

_____

_____

_____

_____

_____

_____

_____

Belief in Modern Times

Therefore I tell you, whatever you ask for in prayer, believe that you have received it, and it will be yours.

(Mark 11:24 NIV)

Our belief is enough for our prayers to be answered. Here is another example of God wanting to answer our prayers. He wants to bless us. We need to believe this. This belief comes from faith, which is another very good reason to ask God to increase our faith.

I have often said, "God, I need a sign that I should do [this]." And I usually get a sign very quickly. Once we were selling a house, and I asked God to let me know if the realtor I was meeting was someone I should hire. I had an impression of roses. The woman was someone from a national agency, but when she got to our meeting, I discovered that she now worked for the Rose agency! Yep, I hired her on the spot!

I look for what I call telegrams or love notes from God every day. I have asked for healing for someone and seen dramatic results. It is not because of my prayers alone, but because many people were lifting this person in prayer, believing that God would heal them.

Of course, we have to be open to the solution He provides, not the one we expect. Often, we want a specific answer and fail to see the greater blessing that He is providing. I have taken financial prayers to Him, and instead of a lump sum of money coming my way, a better job opened up that paid significantly better than I was previously making.

Today with modern technology, social media, and news at the tips of our fingers, we have to be careful. We're exposed to many beliefs that will try to persuade us that if God does exist, He doesn't bother Himself with day-to-day affairs; that we should help ourselves. My question is "When did God change?" He didn't. No point in history contains an account of God changing. God is the same today as he was the day that Jesus was crucified for our sins.

So if God didn't change, it's our perception of Him that has. As we developed technology and grew in knowledge of science and math, the supernatural grew smaller in our lives. So if you want something, thank God that He is going to provide it. Believe that He wants to bless you. Be open to the blessing being different from what you imagined.

Reflection & Prayer

My prayer:
Lord, You are merciful and loving. There is not another
person on earth that loves me and will bless me as You will.
Thank You that today I can ask and receive just as Jesus
said. Amen.

Your Prayer:

_____

_____

_____

_____

_____

_____

_____

_____

_____

_____

_____

_____

Question to Consider:

Why do you think that people don't believe God wants to bless them?

_____
_____
_____
_____
_____
_____
_____
_____
_____
_____
_____
_____
_____
_____
_____
_____
_____

Let Go of Worry

Do not be anxious about anything, but in every situation, by prayer and petition, with thanksgiving, present your requests to God. And the peace of God, which transcends all understanding, will guard your hearts and your minds in Christ Jesus.
(Philippians 4:6–7 NIV)

I feel that we have become a nation of worriers. It is probably due to the constant bombardment of bad news. But aside from preparing to handle dangerous situations before they occur, there is nothing that we can worry about that will change the future. Go into a movie theater, and note where the exits are; then sit back and relax because worrying won't stop a fire from happening.

I have learned to tell God about my fears and ask for His peace. I open my heart and let faith radiate, reassuring me

139

that someone far bigger than circumstance is in control. I allow the Holy Spirit to fill my heart with the confidence that no matter what might happen today, God has seen it and knows what is in store. He would never send me where He hasn't already prepared the land.

Even if the very worst were to happen, He is with me. If the call comes that a loved one has died, He is there to comfort me. If my possessions are suddenly gone, like Job, I will stay quiet in my faith. I can bear anything if God is with me. But the most important thing to remember is the thousands of times the "what if…" did NOT happen. We tend to focus on the one "what if" that does step into our lives. Instead, focus on the 999 things that didn't happen and give your fears to God.

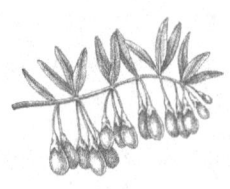

Reflection & Prayer

My prayer:
Dear Lord, today I will have peace and confidence. I will bring all of my anxieties to You. I thank You for all that You have already done for me, which is beyond my understanding. Thank You for guarding my heart and mind in the precious name of Jesus. Amen.

Your Prayer:

_____

_____

_____

_____

_____

_____

_____

_____

_____

_____

Question to Consider:

How does putting your focus on God help you find peace?

_____

_____

_____

_____

_____

_____

_____

_____

_____

_____

_____

_____

_____

_____

_____

_____

Keep Your Spirit Grounded

The sinful nature wants to do evil, which is just the opposite of what the Spirit wants. And the Spirit gives us desires that are the opposite of what the sinful nature desires. These two forces are constantly fighting each other, so you are not free to carry out your good intentions.

(Galatians 5:17 NLT)

We were created with free will; and though God gave us rules to live by, He gives us the choice of whether or not to obey those laws. I know it is difficult to believe that we are born with a sinful nature. Babies aren't sinful, you say. No, but no one has to teach a toddler to lie. So at what point would sin have entered the toddler's life, if not at birth?

The Spirit wants us to choose wisely, to choose those actions that will be pleasing to God— those things that are good, kind, honest, and fair. Our human nature wants to choose that which will promote our ego, lead us further into temptation, and put ourselves ahead of others. It is a constant battle.

We have the Bible, the original owner's manual, as it were. Reading the Bible each day helps to keep our spirit grounded in the light and reminds us of God's love. When we don't feed the good in our soul every day, it becomes weak. We lose the will to make good choices.

My mom noticed when my sisters and I were young that too much time in front of the television led to a laxness in our behavior. Our attention was divided, our responses to her words were slow, and we became rebellious. My mom's solution was to cut the plug off the television. It was a little drastic, but our behaviors improved quickly, and my dad would replace the plug after a few weeks. But each of us had to learn the lesson. By the time we got rid of the television, the cord was a mere eight inches long!

My system was less drastic: I removed the cable box and turned it in. The following month, we may try cable again; but there were whole years that we went without it and the family blossomed. Our daughters' imaginations grew, their behavior improved, and so did their kindness toward each other.

God can remove us from situations that are harmful for us to be in, and we may not realize until years later what an act of protection it was. We need to be mindful of those actions that will take our eyes off God.

Reflection & Prayer

My prayer:
Dear Lord, I know that there are many tempting activities that although not sinful, would put me in a position to make poor choices. I have a sinful nature that goes against what Your Spirit would have me do. Give me the courage to recognize when I am about to go with my natural desires instead of following You. Amen.

Your Prayer:

_____

_____

_____

_____

_____

_____

_____

_____

_____

_____

_____

Question to Consider:

In what ways are you aware of old behaviors fighting for your attention?

_____

_____

_____

_____

_____

_____

_____

_____

_____

_____

_____

_____

_____

_____

_____

_____

Week 4 Review

Luke 8:43–48
Ephesians 4:32
1 Peter 3:9
Mark 11:24
Philippians 4:6–7
Galatians 5:17

Questions to Consider:

1. Which verse had the most impact on you this week?

2. Do these verses change your thoughts on forgiveness? How?

3. How do the choices you make impact your relationship with God?

4. What do these verses tell you about your relationship with God?

_____

_____

5. In what way did your faith grow this week?

_____

_____

6. How will this influence your relationships in the coming week?

_____

_____

7. Review your prayers from this week. How did God speak to you this week?

_____

_____

_____

_____

_____

_____

_____

_____

_____

_____

Thoughts This Week

_____
_____
_____
_____
_____
_____
_____
_____
_____
_____
_____
_____
_____
_____
_____
_____
_____
_____
_____

The Holy Spirit, Our Guide

Week 5

Day 1

Fruits of the Holy Spirit

But the Holy Spirit produces this kind of fruit in our lives; love, joy, peace, patience, kindness, goodness, faithfulness, gentleness, and self-control. There is no law against these things!
(Galatians 5:22–23 NLT)

Isn't this encouraging? I wasn't raised in the church. The few times I attended growing up I heard about the Ten Commandments and how God punishes those who sin. It seemed like there were more sins than seeds on a strawberry! I was very hesitant to become a Christian because of the judgment I would face.

I was a seventies teenager in the age of drugs, sex, and rock and roll. If I didn't look for God, I wouldn't have to look at my life. But one night, that life led to a darkness of wanting to give up. I cried out to God that I couldn't live

153

this life anymore. As I walked down a dirt road in the middle of a thunderstorm, I told God, He might as well just let the flashing lightning strike me down. It didn't happen. Instead, I was filled with peace and a sense of love, so real it felt like a velvet blanket on my skin. But I didn't know anyone that could tell me about God, so I wandered on aimlessly for several more years.

When I did find a place with believers, I was worried that as a new Christian I wouldn't be able to measure up to God's standard. As I explored God's Word and learned more about Him, I found that there were so many wonderful things that He wanted us to experience. I remembered my night of feeling so lost and alone and thought about how the fruits of His Spirit had comforted me.

As we grow and study the Bible, the Holy Spirit talks to our spirit, and the fruits begin to develop in us. We begin to put aside those traits that separate us from God and cultivate the fruits of the Spirit. Keep talking to God and allow yourself to feel this growth within your own spirit as you continue to foster that loving relationship with the Lord.

Reflection & Prayer

My prayer:
Father, Your goodness shines before me. Before I learned
of the fruits of the Spirit, You showed me love, joy, peace,
patience, kindness, goodness, faithfulness, gentleness, and
self-control. Help me to grow in the fruits so that others may
know Your goodness. Amen.

Your Prayer:

_____

_____

_____

_____

_____

_____

_____

_____

_____

_____

Question to Consider:

What does this verse tell you about God?

Day 2

Welcoming the Holy Spirit

But the fruit of the Spirit is love, joy, peace, forbearance, kindness, goodness, faithfulness, gentleness and self-control. Against such things there is no law.

(Galatians 5:22–23 NIV)

As we grow in our faith, we begin to exhibit the fruits of the Spirit more strongly. As our knowledge of God increases, so does the way we respond to others. I was never a particularly harsh person. As a teenager, I would speak without thinking; but unless it was to one of my sisters, I was never intentionally unkind. That didn't mean that others weren't hurt by something I said or did, but rather, I was unaware of how what I said or did would affect them.

Once I began to realize how much God loved me, I became more sensitive to others. I regretted things I had done as a teenager. Things that I couldn't apologize for because people had moved and connections had been lost. I began to take joy in small things and try to bring joy to others.

Standing in a grocery line, I would remark on the cashier's easy attitude or another customer's piece of jewelry. Anything to bring a smile to someone who may not have heard something encouraging all week.

Peace came in a lessening of fears, of which I had more than my share: heights, elevators, bridges, going somewhere by myself, and disappointing others. As I began trusting God, I no longer lived in fear. God replaced my fears with courage. I saw that there was nothing that I was facing alone.

Others began to notice a difference in me. They remarked on how much more they enjoyed being around me because I was a happier person, and less critical of myself and others. I enjoyed myself! I was more relaxed, finding happiness in the everyday. The tenseness of judging myself was replaced with new contentment.

Practice starting each day by welcoming the Holy Spirit. Take a few minutes to deeply breathe in and out. Give thanks for a new day and for the help God has sent you, to walk through it with you. Allow the peace of the Holy Spirit to saturate your being so that you can appreciate the unique person that you are and how very much God loves you.

Reflection & Prayer

My prayer:
Dear Lord, thank You for the security and love You have given me. I was a nervous wreck before I knew You. I am calm because Your peace fills me. I have joy because of all You have given me. I feel Your love all around and I am able to show that love to others. Amen.

Your Prayer:

_____

_____

_____

_____

_____

_____

_____

_____

_____

_____

_____

Question to Consider:

In what ways are you experiencing the love, joy, and peace of the Holy Spirit?

Day 3

The Gift of Forbearance

But the fruit of the Spirit is love, joy, peace, forbearance, kindness, goodness, faithfulness, gentleness and self-control. Against such things there is no law.
(Galatians 5:22–23 NIV)

I had to look up the word forbearance because it isn't commonly used now. It means "patient self-control; restraint and tolerance." Ah, He means teachers! Why didn't God just say the teacher quality? Forbearance should have been issued with the homework assignments to parents that were homeschooling during the quarantine of 2020. Some parents homeschool by choice, and I admire them. But during quarantine, there were millions of parents muddling through days of lessons when they hadn't signed up for that part of parenthood. Not everyone can be a teacher.

A person that has the gifts of forbearance, kindness, and goodness is essential to our society. These are important traits for children to see modeled. Mr. Rogers was a children's television personality who had these qualities. Children watching his show could relax and be children. There was no frantic, constant changing of images or topics. It was a time of gentle, quiet explanation. Things moved slowly.

God has always met my needs. That isn't to say that the answer to my prayers is always "yes". But, whenever I feel that I have messed up, God shows tolerance and offers redemption. For "if we confess our sins, He is faithful and just to forgive our sins and purify us from all unrighteousness" (1 John 1:19). If that doesn't characterize forbearance, kindness, goodness, and faithfulness, I don't know what does.

So, like the ultimate teacher, Jesus, we need to offer patience to those around us, practicing self-control in those moments when we would rather explode with frustration. It is easy to forget that we can control the pace of our lives. We can take the extra seconds to take a deep breath, to change the tone of our voice. We can model the behavior of our Teacher for others.

Reflection & Prayer

My prayer:
Lord, today help me show others the love and kindness
that You show me. There are so many people that need
goodness shown today. Help me to remember to be a faithful
representative of Your love today. Amen.

Your Prayer:

_____

_____

_____

_____

_____

_____

_____

_____

_____

_____

_____

Question to Consider:

How are these traits apparent in your life?

_____

_____

_____

_____

_____

_____

_____

_____

_____

_____

_____

_____

_____

_____

_____

_____

_____

Day 4

Becoming More Like Christ

But the fruit of the Spirit is love, joy, peace, forbearance, kindness, goodness, faithfulness, gentleness and self-control. Against such things there is no law.
(Galatians 5:22—23 NIV)

I think gentleness and self-control are at the tail end of this list because sometimes they are the most difficult to conquer. However, some people are born gentle. Even as babies, they can grab a bee or butterfly without causing damage. I have noticed that the majority of dental hygienists and nurses are gentle as they use very little pressure with their hands. But there are some people, like me, that no matter how hard I concentrate, my touch is not light. When a family member has an injury I want to help, but usually end up causing pain instead of easing it. I will probably never be able to fix that.

But I have learned how to be gentle in speech. I can coach someone out of a job without hurting their feelings. My friend Sue used to tell me that I was good at serving love sandwiches. I could deliver criticism so lovingly that there was no resentment from the other person. I consider this to be a gift I learned from the Holy Spirit. His corrections are always dosed with love. Where my inner voice may attack me for being useless or stupid, the Holy Spirit offers gentle correction and encouragement.

Now self-control is another story. When I get focused on an activity, there is no middle ground. I go full tilt at 100 miles an hour for as long as I can. God and I are working on how I can set limits on my computer time, reading, and phone calls. I am so thankful that our God is loving and patient!

Isn't it wonderful that we can ask the Holy Spirit to show us how to be more Christ-like? God knew that we weren't and can't be perfect so He sent the Holy Spirit to open our hearts and eyes to ways that we can improve. He gave us the will to want to improve. What other gift comes with a built-in desire to use it?

Reflection & Prayer

My prayer:
Lord, remind me today of the power of my actions and how they affect others. I want to be gentle in all interactions and patient with others. Help me, Father, to see when I am so focused on my activity that I miss what is going on around me. Amen.

Your Prayer:

_____

_____

_____

_____

_____

_____

_____

_____

_____

_____

_____

Question to Consider:

Are you gentle by nature? What does this verse tell you about God?

Day 5

Keeping Faith in Times of Great Loss

In the same way, the Spirit helps in our weakness. We do not know what we ought to pray for, but the Spirit himself intercedes for us through wordless groans. And he who searches our hearts knows the mind of the Spirit, because the Spirit intercedes for God's people in accordance with the will of God.

(Romans 8:26–27 NIV)

I take such comfort in these verses. There are times when the grief or pain is too great to verbalize. When a senseless tragedy happens, we are left shocked, unable to comprehend the full extent of what happened and why.

When I lost my sister, Kristi, I was in shock for days. We had no idea if her death was accidental or intentional. She was in a fragile place mentally and had lost hope. I know that I was able to carry on conversations, but I don't remember

169

who I spoke with or how I got on the plane. I was filled with grief and guilt. Was I there for her enough? Was I too insensitive to her pain? I reviewed every conversation and interaction we had had for years, picking at every moment and looking for ways I could have changed the course of events.

Survivor's guilt wants us to take responsibility for things outside our control. Our pain is so intense that we believe there must have been a way to change the outcome. If only... But as I groaned to the Holy Spirit, I was comforted. I may not have had the words to express my pain, but the Holy Spirit interceded for me.

My pain wasn't gone, but I had a fresh understanding of how to accept Kristi's death and continue with my life, focusing on the joys we had shared. I cried while I laughed about how we polkaed in the kitchen while singing "Shall We Dance?" Tears flowed while I smiled about our show tunes duets and silly conversations. I talked with my daughters about the wonderful gifts she made for them. My grief slowly faded into something bearable. My love for her was still there and took precedence in my memory.

Amid tragedy, we are often at a loss for how to pray. But the Holy Spirit knows our hearts. He interprets our pain and confusion and anger and hurt for God. He can take our wordless agony and relate that pain to our Heavenly Father for us. If we trust The Holy Spirit to do that and trust that God knows what we are going through and why; then peace will come. It may not happen immediately. It may be a slow resolution, but by allowing Him to minister to our hearts, peace will come.

Reflection & Prayer

My prayer:
Holy Spirit, thank You for walking with me through those situations too great for me to bear. Thank You for guiding me through that which I don't understand. When my confusion at circumstances is evident, Your presence comforts me. I don't know why this happened, but You do. Be with me as I grow through this. Amen.

Your Prayer:

_____

_____

_____

_____

_____

_____

_____

_____

_____

_____

_____

Question to Consider:

How will this verse help you deal with tragedy?

_____
_____
_____
_____
_____
_____
_____
_____
_____
_____
_____
_____
_____
_____
_____
_____
_____

Day 6

Keeping the Holy Spirit Active in Daily Life

Do not stifle the Holy Spirit. Do not scoff at prophecies, but test everything that is said. Hold on to what is good. Stay away from every kind of evil.

(1 Thessalonians 5:19–22 NLT)

The Holy Spirit is a gift from God. He provides us with knowledge of God and His plan. The Holy Spirit speaks directly to our hearts. Jesus couldn't be everywhere with everyone for all time here on Earth, so He sent the Holy Spirit.

The Holy Spirit gives birth to our spiritual life (John 3:6). The Holy Spirit is the tangible segment of God. We can experience the Holy Spirit in worship, in times of trouble, during prayer, and in the actions of our faith. The Holy Spirit is our direct connection to God, made possible by Jesus Christ.

I certainly don't want to stifle the Holy Spirit. I crave a life full of evidence of the hand of God. I want to feel His presence and know that I am heard and loved; that I am being shown how to walk in righteousness.

As we learn about the fruits of the Spirit and the manifestations of the gifts of the Holy Spirit, we will have a heightened awareness of God. Paul tells us in this epistle not to scoff at prophecies, which are divine words from God, and declare His purposes. They can be for the church or for an individual. And whether used to admonish or comfort, there is a reason that God is sharing this Word. When a word of prophecy is given to you, either by others or for others, test it against Scripture. A true word of prophecy will never go against God's Word. Prophecies, like other gifts, have a season for use. That is, you may receive a word of prophecy that is for the future, not the now.

Hold onto that which is good; treasure it, and store it up in your heart. As with other aspects of life, you can't walk two roads at the same time. To truly encourage the Holy Spirit to be active in your life, choose to turn away from those activities which will lead you into sinful activity.

Reflection & Prayer

My prayer:
Dear Holy Spirit, come reside within me. I welcome Your
presence. Help me to be discerning. Amen.

Your Prayer:

_____

_____

_____

_____

_____

_____

_____

_____

_____

_____

_____

_____

_____

_____

Question to Consider:

In what ways might you stifle the Holy Spirit?

_____
_____
_____
_____
_____
_____
_____
_____
_____
_____
_____
_____
_____
_____
_____
_____

Day 7

Renew Your Mind in the Word

Do not conform to the pattern of this world, but be transformed by the renewing of your mind. Then you will be able to test and approve what God's will is—his good, pleasing and perfect will.
(Romans 12:2 NIV)

Boy, did I need this today! The social media hounds had dragged me through the mud. My opinion was different from theirs, and my feelings were raw by the time I left the conversation. I felt betrayed and hurt, and I wanted to lash out. At one point, I was lectured on the Christian values I was supposed to show. I bit my tongue, and the anger built up. Unresolved anger can become a barrier to relationships.

This reminded me of when my grandmother and her sister got into an argument that neither would back down from. They ended up not speaking for seventy years, even though they lived on the same street. Seventy years! I vowed

I would never be like that. I wouldn't let anger or hurt feelings come between me and the ones I love.

And I won't because I am not to "conform to the pattern of this world". I am to be renewed in my mind by the Word. So I turned to my Bible and was reminded that my source of comfort is in the Lord. His Will is the only one I need to be concerned about.

I realized that by getting drawn into a discussion on social media, I was letting down my guard. I feel that everyone has a right to be heard without criticism whether I agree with them or not. Unfortunately, many don't have that same principle. It is their way or you are wrong, and the venom is unleashed. I feel that the anonymity of social media has led us to believe that people no longer possess feelings that need to be taken into consideration. And it hurts my heart when my first impulse is to respond in kind.

There is an old computer saying, "Garbage in, garbage out." It is true of the human mind also. If it is fed with anger and hate; that is also what fills the heart and is released back to others. My thoughts when I spend too much time on social media turn away from the person I want to be. They become filled with so much anger and false information it's alarming.

So social media, for me, has become a sin. I will police what I read and who I interact with. It is the only way I have to stay in touch with many of my long-distance friends so the list will be pared back to just those.

Just as Satan used an apple to deceive Eve and lead the conversation down a dangerous path, social media can lead us into areas of danger. Whether it is a visual or a conversation that provokes us, we need to be on guard and not allow ourselves to be led into areas of worldly transgressions. Let others fill their hearts and minds with anger and bitterness. We will keep our eyes fixed on God.

Reflection & Prayer

My prayer:
Lord, thank You for reminding me of Your will. Please forgive my anger and bitterness, and show me the better way. Help me to put aside the things of the world that aren't pleasing to You. Amen.

Your Prayer:

_____

_____

_____

_____

_____

_____

_____

_____

_____

_____

_____

_____

Question to Consider:

What patterns of this world draw you away from God?

_____

_____

_____

_____

_____

_____

_____

_____

_____

_____

_____

_____

_____

_____

_____

_____

Week 5 Review

Galatians 5:22–23
Romans 8:26–27
1 Thessalonians 5:19–22
Romans 12:2

Questions to Consider:

1. As you reflect on the fruits of the Holy Spirit, what do they tell you about your relationship with God?

---

2. How can you encourage the growth of the fruits of the Holy Spirit?

---

3. Have you faced times of despair or anger that left you without a way to pray? What would you do now that you know the Lord?

---

4. *In what ways might you stifle the Holy Spirit?*

_____

_____

5. *Review your prayers from this week. How has God spoken to you?*

_____

_____

_____

_____

_____

_____

_____

_____

_____

_____

_____

_____

_____

_____

Thoughts This Week

_____

_____

_____

_____

_____

_____

_____

_____

_____

_____

_____

_____

_____

_____

_____

_____

_____

_____

_____

The Holy Spirit, Our Counselor

Week 6

Exploring Your Spiritual Gifts

There are different kinds of gifts but the same Spirit distributes them. There are different kinds of service, but the same Lord. There are different kinds of working, but in all of them and in everyone it is the same God at work.

(1 Corinthians 12:4–6 NIV)

I get so excited when I think of this! Our world is a wonderful and varied place because we are not all the same. Can you imagine what it would be like if we all had the gift of service, but no one had the gift of healing? Or we all had the gift of wisdom, but no one had the gift of knowledge?

God distributes these gifts through the Holy Spirit. He knows what gift fits our personality. He knows who can handle the gift of prophecy and who is better suited for another gift. You probably have one or more of these but have never considered how they came to you or how God can use them to help others.

As we go through the different types of gifts, think about the situations that you act or react to in positive ways when others don't seem to be able to respond. Think about the ways that others seem to intuitively know what needs to be done while you just shake your head.

That is why it is so important that you find a church or support network that provides ways to develop the gifts of the members. It is for the good of the community that each person knows and appreciates their gifts, as well as those of others. Operating in a sphere you are comfortable in will decrease the stress in your life. We can't be good at everything.

Reflection & Prayer

My prayer:
Father, thank You for surrounding me with people who have gifts that are different from mine. Thank You that I don't have to seek solutions to problems by myself. You are always there and put people in my life that You guide. Help me to be of assistance to others. Amen.

Your Prayer:

_____

_____

_____

_____

_____

_____

_____

_____

_____

_____

_____

Question to Consider:

Do you attend a church that you feel is interested in developing your gifts?

_____

_____

_____

_____

_____

_____

_____

_____

_____

_____

_____

_____

_____

_____

_____

_____

_____

Day 2

The Gift of Wisdom and Knowledge

Now to each one the manifestation of the Spirit is given for the common good. To one there is given through the Spirit a message of wisdom, to another a message of knowledge by means of the same Spirit, to another faith by the same Spirit, to another gifts of healing by the one Spirit, to another miraculous powers, to another prophecy, to another distinguishing between spirits, to another speaking in different kinds of tongues, and to still another the interpretation of tongues.

(1 Corinthians 12:7–10 NIV)

Wisdom is the quality of having experience, knowledge, and good judgment. Knowledge pertains to an awareness or understanding of someone or something, such as facts, information, or skills. Knowledge is having information, and wisdom is putting it to use appropriately. Learning to use knowledge beneficially is part of maturity.

My daughter, Denise, has wisdom. She has four children,

193

and I am amazed at the wisdom she exhibits when dealing with some of the situations that arise. I raised three girls in the '80s. It was a different time for families. Because Denise has sons, she has had to deal with issues like policing online gaming and providing physical outlets, issues that I never encountered. She understands that her children all learn in different ways and chooses the schools that will benefit each.

My daughter, Kelly, has the gift of knowledge. She loves learning and sharing information. Her explanations of passages of literature or the Bible will have you thinking in a new depth with new insight. Her teachers would comment on the joy they got from reading her essays. It validated their instructional efforts.

When Jesus came upon the woman being stoned for adultery, he didn't name names. He looked around at the men with stones in their hands and said, "He who is without sin, cast the first stone" (John 8:2–11). He had knowledge of who had sinned and with whom. But he let their hearts do the talking. The Holy Spirit gives knowledge and wisdom to protect and help us mature in the Word. They are to build up the church. We are called to use our gifts for the good of all.

This week think about your God-given gifts. What does that say about God's purpose for you? How will you use your gift to glorify God?

Reflection & Prayer

My prayer:
Lord, give me wisdom and knowledge. Help me to use these
gifts to benefit and not to harm. Amen.

Your Prayer:

_____

_____

_____

_____

_____

_____

_____

_____

_____

_____

_____

_____

_____

_____

_____

_____

Question to Consider:

How does this help you better understand the Holy Spirit and our relationship with God?

_____

_____

_____

_____

_____

_____

_____

_____

_____

_____

_____

_____

_____

_____

_____

_____

_____

_____

Day 3

The Gift of Faith

A spiritual gift is given to each of us so we can help each other. To one person the Spirit gives the ability to give wise advice; to another the same Spirit gives a message of special knowledge. The same Spirit gives great faith to another, and to someone else the Spirit gives the gift of healing. He gives one person the power to perform miracles and another the ability to prophesy. He gives someone else the ability to discern whether a message is from the Spirit of God or from another spirit. Still another person is given the ability to speak in unknown languages, while another is given the ability to interpret what is being said.

(1 Corinthians 12:7–10 NLT)

The Holy Spirit gives us the gift of faith. When our faith is small or we aren't sure if we have the faith that is needed to trust God with something really big, all we need to do is ask. I have called upon God on several occasions to give me more faith. To make my faith as big as a boulder because I had no choice but to trust him with the life of another.

Our youngest daughter, Kelly, had appendicitis as a two-year-old. The doctors didn't believe a toddler could have appendicitis, so she had to endure a more invasive procedure to verify it. I wasn't allowed in the room. I was in an adjoining room, listening to my baby scream, unable to do anything except cry and pray. It was one of the most horrific moments of my life. I prayed for faith. Faith to trust God with the life of my baby. I admitted that I had no control and she was in God's hands. Immediately I was filled with peace. I knew with deep assurance that she would be fine, no matter what ensued from that moment on.

Her appendix had ruptured during the procedure, and she was rushed into surgery. The surgeon said that there was damage and infection spilled out into her abdominal cavity. He wasn't sure after surgery how she would do. But I was sure! God had given me peace and the faith to trust Him. I learned at that time that God is big enough to handle anything I will trust Him with.

I am not saying that God will never give us anything too big for us to handle. I believe that when He does, it is an opportunity for growth in our faith because we have to rely on Him and not the world or our own devices.

By incorporating prayer and faith into our daily life it will be second nature to turn to God when life is tough. Think about how you want to act and react during all the moments in your life this week, and how you will include God. Try to identify the times when God has given you the faith to cope with a crisis.

Reflection & Prayer

My prayer:
Father, thank You that I have the Holy Spirit to be with me and give me faith. Thank You that You will always provide what I need when I ask. Be with me today, and enlarge my faith. Let others see my faith and confidence and be drawn to You. Amen.

Your Prayer:

_____

_____

_____

_____

_____

_____

_____

_____

_____

_____

_____

Question to Consider:

What does this say to you about how the Holy Spirit can work in your life?

_____

_____

_____

_____

_____

_____

_____

_____

_____

_____

_____

_____

_____

_____

_____

_____

The Gift of Healing

Now to each one the manifestation of the Spirit is given for the common good. To one there is given through the Spirit a message of wisdom, to another a message of knowledge by means of the same Spirit, to another faith by the same Spirit, to another gifts of healing by the one Spirit, to another miraculous powers, to another prophecy, to another distinguishing between spirits, to another speaking in different kinds of tongues, and to still another the interpretation of tongues.

(1 Corinthians 12:7–10 NIV)

My daughter Megan has the gift of healing and organization. She is a nurse; and if an accident happens, she immediately springs into action, prioritizing and assessing. I don't have those gifts. I hate the smell of blood. Ugh! But Megan's nursing gifts in the labor and delivery department aren't limited to medical. She has sat with grieving parents as they said goodbye to their babies. She has a soothing spirit that calms them and validates their baby's short life. I consider this an extension of her gift of healing. Her spirit communes with the spirits of the parents as she sits and cries with them. Whether the gift of healing is spontaneous and miraculous healing or ministering to wounded souls, it is a gift from the Holy Spirit. A gift that brings God's presence into the moment. Sitting with those who are dying and consoling those who are wounded in spirit, those who have been injured physically or mentally—these are all examples of the gift of healing.

When we believe in the Holy Spirit and invite him into our hearts, there is no limit to the work that can be accomplished. God is as active now as He was in the New Testament. In my mind, the only restriction to miracles is our lack of faith. We have replaced faith in His ability to perform miracles with one of science and reason. I have seen healings accelerated by the Holy Spirit. There are countless accounts of people in the end stages of cancer who have been miraculously healed. Our God hasn't changed. Our capacity for miracles has.

Today, believe with your whole heart in God's miracles. If you are available, God will use you. Be bold. Go out into your day or night with the confidence that the Holy Spirit will bring people into your life that you can help, be it with healing words or actions. Be a blessing to those around you, as well as to yourself.

Reflection & Prayer

My prayer:
Father, Your presence brings peace and healing to our
weary souls. You are with us when we lie injured and in grief.
Thank You for people that can communicate Your healing
and peace to those who need it. Amen.

Your Prayer:

_____

_____

_____

_____

_____

_____

_____

_____

_____

_____

_____

_____

_____

Question to Consider:

What does this gift tell you about God?

_____
_____
_____
_____
_____
_____
_____
_____
_____
_____
_____
_____
_____
_____
_____

The Gift of Prophecy and Discernment

A spiritual gift is given to each of us so we can help each other. To one person the Spirit gives the ability to give wise advice; to another the same Spirit gives a message of special knowledge. The same Spirit gives great faith to another, and to someone else the Spirit gives the gift of healing. He gives one person the power to perform miracles and another the ability to prophesy. He gives someone else the ability to discern whether a message is from the Spirit of God or from another spirit. Still another person is given the ability to speak in unknown languages, while another is given the ability to interpret what is being said.

(1 Corinthians 12:7–10 NLT)

I found that when I first started as a Christian, my faith placed limits on God because I didn't understand His immense being. It takes a while, doesn't it, to expand our mind to His capabilities? Of course, we know on some level that He is capable of anything— He created the Earth, after all. But we live in the age of technology and scientific explanation. We are cynical and look for the trick in the magic.

The Holy Spirit enables us to step forward and do the improbable or what some may consider impossible. I have heard stories of pregnant women who were able to lift a car off a loved one. Or people that were at the scene of a horrific accident and later had no idea how they were able to extricate the victim. Miraculous powers include anything that is beyond human ability or comprehension. And our God is mighty! With Him all things are possible.

Prophecy is a gift that I suspect many have but don't acknowledge. They have dreams or feelings and attribute them to coincidence or "second sight." While in prayer in 2001, I was given a vision of two huge skyscrapers on fire. I was crying for all the people inside, and God assured me that each had an opportunity to know and accept Him. Two months later, I watched in horror as flames erupted in the World Trade Center towers. I don't know how I could have used this knowledge in any way except to comfort those that were grieving and assure them of God's love and faithfulness.

Prophecy is meant to be used for the building up of the church. The prophets of the Old Testament foretold of the coming of the Messiah. It was to give hope to the Jews as they lived through times of tribulation and to warn them of the consequences of not following God. Those who have the gift of discerning spirits recognize the spirit of others. They can sense the good or evil in others without a word spoken. Many pastors have the gift of discerning spirits to protect their congregations. Should someone try to disrupt a service or cause dissension within the church, the pastor and elders should be the ones able to recognize something unholy at work and put an end to it.

Learning to listen to our hearts is so important. The Holy Spirit is the way God warns us of danger and uplifts us. Discernment is how the Holy Spirit keeps us safe. The more we know of Scripture, the easier it is to discern when someone is trying to mislead us. As we write out our prayers we often find words of prophecy. This week record those feelings and thoughts that may pertain to future actions.

Reflection & Prayer

My prayer:
Father, help me to recognize and accept when the Holy Spirit is gifting me with one of these. Give me the courage to develop and use these gifts for the good of others so that they might see You in my life. Help me to remember to give You the glory in all things. Amen.

Your Prayer:

_____

_____

_____

_____

_____

_____

_____

_____

_____

_____

_____

_____

Question to Consider:

How does God use these gifts to enable those who believe in Him?

_____

_____

_____

_____

_____

_____

_____

_____

_____

_____

_____

_____

_____

_____

_____

The Gift of Tongues

Now to each one the manifestation of the Spirit is given for the common good. To one there is given through the Spirit a message of wisdom, to another a message of knowledge by means of the same Spirit, to another faith by the same Spirit, to another gifts of healing by the one Spirit, to another miraculous powers, to another prophecy, to another distinguishing between spirits, to another speaking in different kinds of tongues, and to still another the interpretation of tongues.

(1 Corinthians 12:7–10 NIV)

I have found that these gifts are among the most difficult to accept for some Christians. They want nothing to do with something so far outside their comprehension as if in some way the gift of tongues will be out of their control. Many churches accept only that this is the gift of languages. While the gift of speaking and understanding other languages (Acts 2:4–11) may be within these gifts, I believe that tongues refer

211

to a special way of communicating with God through the Holy Spirit.

I was part of a church that believed and practiced the gifts of the Holy Spirit. One thing that the pastor said was that there was no reason to get squirrelly with them—that is, to pretend that you have no control. We have control over every gift and can decide whether or not to use it.

If having the gift of tongues simply meant uncontrollable utterances, then all of the other gifts would be outside our control. Ours is a God of control, not chaos. There is no halfway with some gifts being subject to our restraint and others not. This isn't a gift to be feared; for it, like all gifts, is from the Holy Spirit. When someone uses a prayer language or tongues in church, there should always be an interpretation, or someone who has the ability to distinguish if the message and the spirit of the speaker is godly or not. God doesn't want us to be led into confusion by these gifts. The Holy Spirit is here to teach and guide us in truth. Most people I know use tongues as a prayer language. It is only between them and God, allowing the Holy Spirit to put into words what we can't.

Today embrace your gifts, do not fear them. God has given this gift to you for a reason. Accept yourself and accept others with their own unique gifts. This is how God has planned this for us. Allow this to give you the peace you need today to move forward and use your gift.

Reflection & Prayer

My prayer:
Dear Lord, help me to understand these gifts of the Holy Spirit. Help me to see why You choose to use these gifts to help us. Help me be open to understanding all of the gifts, not just a few. Amen.

Your Prayer:

_____

_____

_____

_____

_____

_____

_____

_____

_____

_____

_____

_____

Question to Consider:

How has your perception of the gifts of the Holy Spirit changed?

_____

_____

_____

_____

_____

_____

_____

_____

_____

_____

_____

_____

_____

_____

_____

_____

_____

_____

The Truth of Blasphemy

I tell you the truth, all sin and blasphemy can be forgiven, but anyone who blasphemes the Holy Spirit will never be forgiven. This is a sin with eternal consequences.

(Mark 3:28–29 NLT)

Blasphemy is the act of insulting, showing contempt, or displaying a lack of reverence for God. Blasphemy can be in words or actions. Anytime a sacred article or holy place is defiled, an article is written claiming that man has the same capabilities as God, or a person declares themselves equal to God, we are seeing blasphemy in action.

We have seen the blasphemy of many sacred places and articles in recent years. Temples were desecrated, the name of God taken in vain, churches broken into, and altars defiled. And this verse says that as heinous as these crimes are, they can be forgiven. But to blaspheme the Holy Spirit is unforgivable.

And why would this one offense have eternal consequences? Our bodies are holy temples in which the Holy Spirit resides. The Holy Spirit is our guide and brings the truth of the mercy and grace of God into our hearts. If we are continually rejecting the guidance of the Holy Spirit, there is a hardening of our hearts. A turning of our backs on the knowledge of God is a rejection of the salvation of Jesus Christ. This is a consistent rejection of God, a denial of his existence.

We all have moments of being angry with God and lashing out at Him, of rejecting a gift from the Holy Spirit. These don't constitute blasphemy of the Holy Spirit. These acts are forgivable when a contrite heart turns to God and asks for forgiveness. As I have read many times, if you are worried that you have blasphemed the Holy Spirit, you probably haven't. That worry represents a heart tender to the Lord.

Reflection & Prayer

My prayer:
Holy Spirit, thank You for Your presence in my life and heart.
Please forgive me for any act that grieves You. Keep my
heart tender toward You, always aware of Your guidance.
Amen.

Your Prayer:

_____

_____

_____

_____

_____

_____

_____

_____

_____

_____

_____

_____

Question to Consider:

What does this verse tell you about God?

_____
_____
_____
_____
_____
_____
_____
_____
_____
_____
_____
_____
_____
_____
_____
_____

Week 6 Review

1 Corinthians 12:4–6
1 Corinthians 12:7–10
Mark 3:28–29

Questions to Consider:

1. This week we examined the gifts of the Holy Spirit. What are the gifts of the Holy Spirit?

_____

_____

2. What do these gifts tell you about the love of God?

_____

3. What do you believe your gift is?

_____

_____

4. *How can you exercise your gift and grow in it?*

_____

_____

_____

5. *How does God use these gifts to enable you to share your faith?*

_____

_____

6. *Review your prayers from this week. How has God spoken to you?*

_____

_____

_____

_____

_____

_____

_____

_____

_____

_____

Thoughts This Week

_____
_____
_____
_____
_____
_____
_____
_____
_____
_____
_____
_____
_____
_____
_____
_____
_____
_____

Our Daily Life

Week 7

Day 1

Seizing Blessed Opportunities

And when the Lord sent you from Kadesh-barnea, saying, "Go up and occupy the land that I have given you," you rebelled against the command of the Lord your God, neither trusting him or obeying him.

(Deuteronomy 9:23 NRSV)

Kadesh-barnea means "holiness" or "separateness" according to Biblical Archeology. This is the place where the Israelites stopped before entering the promised land. When Joshua and Caleb explored the promised land, they found the land bountiful, as the Lord had promised; but it was ruled by the Amorites. The Israelites grumbled about the height and strength of the Amorites and refused to take the land.

This is the first time I have thought of my comfort as a form of rebellion. How many times have we refused a larger blessing because we are comfortable with the one we have?

It is scary to step out in faith. It usually requires a measure of faith that is bigger than we have. It definitely means allowing God to stretch us past our comfort zone.

There were times in my life that were like doors of opportunity sliding open. And like sliding doors, these special moments were only accessible for a short time. If I stepped through, I was blessed. There was no penalty per se for not accepting the opportunity, except for a lack of growth. I didn't lose anything, but I also missed out on the blessing of something greater. Your promptings will be tailored to you. It may be working with the homeless, on the mission field, starting a new business, doing motivational speaking, or beginning a new career. I can guarantee that whatever the Lord is leading you to, whatever land He has prepared, will be a blessing much bigger than your current situation. Whatever it is, be bold because the Lord will be with you while you are slaying the giants of doubt and opposition. As my friend Donna says, "Don't let the comfort zone of your past limit the potential of your future."

Reflection & Prayer

My prayer:
Dear Lord, has there been a time when You sought to send me out of a place of separateness; a place where I was protected and refused to leave? I know that if You are sending me, then the way has been prepared. Please help me to trust and obey Your promptings. Help me to take risks as You guide me in growth and blessing. Help me to step out of the zone of comfort I have created and into the land of limitless possibilities that You have prepared for me. Amen.

Your Prayer:

_____

_____

_____

_____

_____

_____

_____

_____

_____

Question to Consider:

Is there an object of comfort (rebellion) that is stopping you from growing closer to God?

_____

_____

_____

_____

_____

_____

_____

_____

_____

_____

_____

_____

_____

_____

_____

_____

Don Your Spiritual Armor

Stand firm then with the belt of truth buckled around your waist, with the breastplate of righteousness in place and with your feet fitted with the readiness that comes from the gospel of peace. In addition to all this, take up the shield of faith, with which you can extinguish all the flaming arrows of the evil one. Take the helmet of salvation and the sword of the Spirit, which is the word of God.
(Ephesians 6:14–17 NIV)

The armor described would have brought to mind that of a Roman soldier. Roman soldiers were trained to fight as part of a conquering machine. Their armor was designed to ensure success by protecting vulnerable parts of the body, just as the individual pieces of the Armor of God are meant to ensure our protection and our victory in spiritual warfare.

The belt kept the armor together and held the sword. When the belt was put in place, the soldier was ready for battle. Our belt of God's truth protects us from the lies of the enemy. When our lives are based on truth we are less susceptible to temptation and deception.

The belt of truth holds firm the breastplate of righteousness. Just as the Roman breastplate protects not only the chest and stomach area but also the side and back from any hit that may get past the shield, our righteousness comes from obeying God's Word. When we live under God's instructions our hearts and souls are protected. The enemy is unable to lead us astray with unseen attacks.

Roman soldiers' sandals had spikes on the bottom to grip the ground. When their feet were planted, they were anchored to the ground. They also had thick soles and leather straps that protected their ankles and the tendons in their heel. These sandals were made for long marches and battles. Our peace, through the forgiveness of sins, brings us a closeness to God that makes us immovable. We stand secure in His Love and Faithfulness.

Roman shields were made of wood, leather, canvas, and metal. It could be soaked in water to protect against fiery arrows. When they were going into battle as a unit, those on the outer edges held their shields against their bodies to protect the front, rear, and sides. Those in the middle held their shields overhead to stop any rocks or arrows from penetrating above. Our shield of faith allows us to believe that God will answer our prayers. We can ask in absolute belief that He hears us and there is nothing that we cannot request, no miracle that we cannot believe in because our God is mightier than any being that may attack us. His protection is total.

The Romans were like armored beetles advancing on

their enemy. The helmet protected the head and guarded the eyes, nose, ears, and mouth. Our helmet of salvation protects our minds from deception and sin.

Our ultimate piece of weaponry is the sword of the Spirit, which is the Word of God. The Holy Spirit resides within us, our direct link to the Voice of God, guiding and comforting us at all times.

Now take this image and apply it to the weapons of God. Visualize these mighty spiritual weapons as protection for our minds, hearts, and souls. We have the promise of the gospel and the Holy Spirit. And when we connect with other believers, we are a strong unit. Let's not forget our faith. The gospel of peace makes us true conquerors, for it offers the greatest truth there is.

The closer you draw to God, the harder the enemy will fight to separate you from His Grace. Remember to wear your spiritual armor; rely on God to provide a way to withstand temptation. (1 Cor 10:13) God has given us the weapons we need for spiritual battle. We need only use them.

Reflection & Prayer

My prayer:
Dear Lord, I want to stand firm in Your truth today. Help me to stand on Your Word, trusting in it to protect my heart, mind, and soul. I want to live in righteousness, blameless in action and word. Your Word gives me peace and confidence. I will use my faith to advance into areas that might otherwise scare me. I know that the enemy will try to use those closest to me to hurt me or cause me shame. Using my faith in You, I will look for the source behind their actions. I will try to understand their fear or injured pride and believe that it is a thing that I can bring to You. Thank You, Father, that I have others to stand with me when I am weak or uncertain, to pray with and for me. For if You are for me, who can be against me? Amen.

Your Prayer:

_____

_____

_____

_____

_____

_____

_____

Question to Consider:

How does the visual description of the armor of God help you understand this verse?

_____

_____

_____

_____

_____

_____

_____

_____

_____

_____

_____

_____

_____

_____

Day 3

Fighting Daily Battles

Finally, be strong in the Lord and in the strength of his power.
Put on the whole armor of God, so that you may be able to stand
against the wiles of the devil. For our struggle is not against
enemies of blood and flesh, but against the rulers, against the
authorities, against the cosmic powers of this present darkness,
against the spiritual forces of evil in the heavenly places.

(Ephesians 6:10–12 NRSV)

Whoa now! Those are some big names, real heavy
hitters! But they are nothing compared to the power of
God. And we have a mighty arsenal of weapons. We have
the armor of God (Eph. 6:13–17). We possess the truth,
righteousness, faith, salvation, the Holy Spirit, and the
gospel of peace. We tend to forget to think of our daily
struggles as battles.

When a family member betrays a trust or wounds you, do
you consider how the enemy might be using those closest to

you to inflict pain? If a coworker uses your idea to impress your boss, what is your reaction? When someone cuts you off in traffic just as you are praising the Lord in song, do you have choice words for that person or recognize it as a flaming arrow? It is easy to stand firm when we see it coming, but that isn't usually the way attacks work, is it?

The enemy will use others or ourselves to demean, condemn, and slice away at our conviction. Recently, I remembered Vacation Bible School, where I gave my life to Jesus. I was full of hope and joy and peace. There was excitement over a discovery that I had never before experienced. But when I got home, the enemy started.

"Really? Do you even know what that means?" my mom asked. I was eight and completely forgot what I had just learned. I was immediately deflated.

In yesterday's devotional, we learned about putting on the armor of God every day to combat these spiritual battles. The enemy doesn't want us drawing closer to God. We need to be ever mindful that doubts and condemnation are from the enemy, not God. Our God knew us before we were born. His plans are to prosper and not to harm us (Jeremiah 29:11).

Reflection & Prayer

My prayer:
Lord, help me to remember to wear Your armor today and every day. Give me the forethought to identify the source of my attacks and refuse to yield. Help me to be strong in You and in the strength of Your power. When I am feeling defeated, help me to take solace in Your Word. Fill me with the conviction that I am Your daughter, that I am loved and protected. Help me to be bold in reaching out to others and bringing them to a place of safety and peace in You. Whether the enemy attacks my pride, my physical or mental health, or my emotions, remind me that You are my refuge. And with You, I am sheltered. Amen.

Your Prayer:

_____

_____

_____

_____

_____

_____

_____

_____

Question to Consider:

How does this help you to identify ways you might be coming under attack?

_____

_____

_____

_____

_____

_____

_____

_____

_____

_____

_____

_____

_____

_____

_____

Day 4

Becoming a Conqueror

No, in all these things we are more than conquerors through him who loved us.

(Romans 8:37 NRSV)

More than conquerors... more than conquerors. A conqueror overcomes an adversary or wins a country in war. Jesus overcame the adversary when he was crucified for our sins. He overcame the punishment of eternal death and eternal separation from our Lord. He died for us. When we accept Jesus Christ as our Lord and Savior, we become more than conquerors.

I am in the process of learning to live as a conqueror. Are you? I want to claim dominance over things that trouble me. My sister, Kathy, is a conqueror with a capital C! She lets nothing stand between her and whatever she sees as a blessing from God. Once, my car was stolen with her new

Christmas dishes in the trunk. She demanded that Satan return my car and her dishes unscathed immediately. Within thirty minutes, we received the call that the car (and dishes) had been found. She lives this verse!

And why not? This is our promise. When someone is being impatient in the grocery line, I can pray for them and then take control of my reactions by turning the conversation to them, their smile, their earrings, or their shirt. Stop the negativity right there. After all, most people just need some kindness in their life. I don't know what burdens they are carrying. Here, I can be a conqueror.

I strive to conquer my attitude in traffic or while dealing with customer service representatives. I pray for those that have hurt me. These are small steps that get us into the habit of expecting more, like a healed relationship, a broken habit, or the return of a stolen item. We are meant to be more than conquerors. We are meant to overcome the adversary in spiritual combat. That is why we are reminded to put on the armor of God (Eph. 6:13).

Reflection & Prayer

My prayer:
Father, give me eyes to see and a heart to discern when I am coming under spiritual attack. Lead me to victory over daily small struggles as I learn to fight bigger battles. Help me to include others in my victory, Lord, by recognizing when someone is in pain. Prompt me when to pray for and with them, Father, that they too may overcome sadness, depression, loneliness, and hurt. Remind me to pray for the protection of others even if I don't think they deserve it; for You offered me protection, forgiveness, and grace unmerited. Amen.

Your Prayer:

_____

_____

_____

_____

_____

_____

_____

_____

Question to Consider:

What is one way that you could be more than a conqueror today?

_____

_____

_____

_____

_____

_____

_____

_____

_____

_____

_____

_____

_____

_____

_____

Day 5

Do Not Be Misled

The men said "This is the day the Lord spoke of when he said to
you, 'I will give your enemy into your hands for you to deal with as
you wish.'" Then David crept up unnoticed and cut off a corner of
Saul's robe.

(1 Samuel 24:4 NIV)

David's men weren't as sensitive to the voice of God
as David himself was. They used the words of the Lord to
convince him that this is the right thing to do. And David
allowed himself to be swayed by their words. Here was Saul,
the king, standing at the entrance to the cave where David
and his men were hiding. Outside was Saul's army, intent
on capturing and killing David. Of course, David is going to
consider taking advantage of the situation to put one over on
Saul. "Look, Saul! While you were relieving yourself, I was
able to creep up and cut a corner off your robe! I could have
killed you, but I didn't." What a way to make Saul look bad in

front of his troops!

Scripture has been used to justify many crimes—from abuse to slavery, from the Spanish Inquisition to the Salem Witch Trials. The devil used Scripture to tempt Jesus. How often in history have people been harmed because the leaders stood with "the right of God" on their side? It is so difficult to stand alone in the heat of drama. We can tap into divine wisdom by asking the Holy Spirit to bring the Word alive. The Holy Spirit gives us the truth and wisdom from God so we may have true understanding. This is why it is so important to read the Bible. We must know what it says to be armed to combat its misuse.

For most of history, much of the population was illiterate. They had to rely on what the church leaders said was in the Bible because they couldn't read it for themselves. When someone quotes the Bible and their stance doesn't seem to line up with what I know of God, I check it by reading the entire chapter. Putting verses in context is the best way to ensure that we are not being misled.

Reflection & Prayer

My prayer:
Holy Spirit, teach me today how to discern the truth. Remind me that the meaning of learning Scripture is to develop my walk with the Lord, not to harm or condemn others. Show me how to use my knowledge to defend and protect those who are being wronged. Give me the courage to speak out when I know the wrongness of a situation. Let me be a beacon for God's Word, not a tool used to demean or defeat others. Amen.

Your Prayer:

_____

_____

_____

_____

_____

_____

_____

_____

_____

Question to Consider:

Can you think of a time that Scripture was used to endorse something that you felt was wrong?

Day 6

Cultivating Your Heart

The men said "This is the day the Lord spoke of when he said to you, 'I will give your enemy into your hands for you to deal with as you wish.'" Then David crept up unnoticed and cut off a corner of Saul's robe. Afterward, David was conscience-stricken for having cut off a corner of his robe. He said to his men, "The Lord forbid that I should do such a thing to my master, the Lord's anointed, or lay my hand on him; for he is the anointed of the Lord." With these words David sharply rebuked his men and did not allow them to attack Saul. And Saul left the cave and went his way.

(1 Samuel 24:4–7 NIV)

How is cutting off the corner of a robe a violation of what the Lord had told David? I was puzzled by this. Saul was in the cave relieving himself. David snuck up on Saul while he was in a very vulnerable position. Saul was leading 3,000 men on a search to capture and kill David. David took a corner of Saul's robe instead of killing him. So where is the harm?

I think David was conscience-stricken because this is splitting hairs. God said that David was forbidden from laying his hands on Saul. Whether it is a piece of clothing or harming the man, David was forbidden. Wrong is wrong. An infraction is the same in God's eye as a felony.

So cutting a corner of the robe is the same as killing the man. David was told not to harm Saul, not to harm the Lord's anointed. Here David intended to embarrass Saul in front of his men. Isn't this causing harm?

How often do we cut corners, make fun of someone, or correct them publicly? That is unkindness. Buying a product that is priced wrong? That is stealing. Quoting just enough scripture to support an opinion? That is lying by omission. Asking for prayer while divulging hurtful information? That is gossiping. We could think of a million little infractions that amount to the same thing: not following the greatest commands—to love the Lord your God with all your heart, all your soul, and all your mind, and to love your neighbor as yourself. Let's work to cultivate a heart as tender to the Word of the Lord as King David had.

Reflection & Prayer

My prayer:
Open the eyes of my heart today, Lord, that I may be aware of where I am cutting corners, of following only the letter of the law. Let my heart feel the truth of scripture, Holy Spirit. Give me discernment. Let me hear my words as You hear them. Let me see my actions as You see them. Let me see others through Your eyes, Lord, that I may be fully aware of them and the love You have for them. Amen.

Your Prayer:

_____

_____

_____

_____

_____

_____

_____

_____

_____

_____

_____

Question to Consider:

What are the consequences of cutting corners for yourself?
For others?

_____

_____

_____

_____

_____

_____

_____

_____

_____

_____

_____

_____

_____

_____

_____

Day 7

Find Your Spiritual Warriors

Be joyful in hope, patient in affliction, faithful in prayer.
(Romans 12:12 NIV)

I miss my Bible study friends when we are apart. When we are together, there is wisdom, joy, contemplation, and fullness in my spirit, due to the presence of the Holy Spirit. Being with others that love God and speak of His goodness recharges my batteries.

I pray that you know someone like my friend Nancy. Spending time with her is like a super long hug. She rejoices in the Lord and speaks of Him and His works. I leave her with a love bucket full to overflowing. Nancy is one of the people that I would want to be with in times of affliction. Her unwavering faith and sweetness would elevate even the direst situation. It's not that Nancy wouldn't recognize the seriousness, but her faith is solid—it can be felt. I am sure that Nancy has pains in her life; but to her, God is large, strong, and all encompassing. She is someone that I thank God for; a reminder of His faithfulness and love.

Building relationships, whether through Bible studies or church, increase our knowledge of God and uplifts us. When afflictions strike, these are the people who will pray for and stand with you. These are the people you can sit silently with while they grieve or intercede for in times of conflict. You can offer strength, be the pillar they can lean on when overcome by adversity, and remind them of the faithfulness of God.

Reflection & Prayer

My prayer:
Father, things may look bad today, but You are there. You are protecting me, surrounding me with love, and giving me hope. I will be patient as I await the outcome, sure that Your plans for me are better than I could imagine. I will be joyful in all things, You use all things to work for the good of those who love You. Thank You for our Christian family, those who share our faith and remind us of Your faithfulness. Amen.

Your Prayer:

_____

_____

_____

_____

_____

_____

_____

_____

_____

_____

Question to Consider:

How can you use this verse to encourage others?

_____
_____
_____
_____
_____
_____
_____
_____
_____
_____
_____
_____
_____
_____
_____
_____
_____

Week 7 Review

Deuteronomy 9:23
Ephesians 6:14–17
Ephesians 6:10–12
Romans 8:37
1 Samuel 24:4–7
Romans 12:12

Questions to Consider:

1. This week we talked about rebellion and combat, stepping out of our comfort zones, and standing firm in our faith. Did you recognize an area in which you were rebelling or cutting corners?

_____

_____

_____

2. How might you be missing out on a greater blessing by not stepping forward in faith?

_____

_____

3. Had you previously considered the spiritual forces that are used to fight against our faith?

_____

_____

4. How does the enemy use those we love to bring a spiritual attack against us?

_____

_____

5. How can we discern if a biblical reference is being used properly?

_____

_____

6. Review your prayers this week. What has God said to you?

_____

_____

_____

_____

_____

_____

_____

_____

Thoughts This Week

Our Relationships

Week 8

Day 1

You Are Never Alone

So Jacob served seven years to get Rachel, but they seemed like only a few days to him because of his love for her. Then Jacob said to Laban, "Give me my wife. My time is completed, and I want to make love to her." So Laban brought together all the people of the place and gave a feast. But when evening came, he took his daughter Leah and brought her to Jacob, and Jacob made love to her.

(Genesis 29:20–23 NIV)

How did Leah feel? On the one hand, Leah would have been ecstatic to be marrying the man she loved, but how hurtful it must be to be thought so worthless that you are fobbed off on an unsuspecting bridegroom on the wedding night! How weary she must have been of being compared (and found wanting) to Rachel. Rachel was beautiful, and all we are told about Leah is that she had either lovely eyes (NRSV) or weak eyes (NIV). Merely a piece of property to be disposed of in a dishonest transaction. And Rachel becomes the favorite wife the next week!

Leah was truly a woman of strength, faith, and hope. She loved Jacob and never gave up trying to win his affection. Leah strove to be pleasing to Jacob. You can see it in the progression of names she gives her sons, but it is the Lord who hears and rewards her. I don't think she ever earned Jacob's love. She did, however, have the love of one who never fails. The Lord heard her and blessed her. He sees our hearts and knows our pain. He rewarded Leah's patience and determination.

When I think about it, Leah was really quite remarkable in her ability to stand firm in her faith. While she may have cried out to the Lord, she never blamed Him for her circumstances. Rather she relied on Him to change them or change her. I wonder if I would have handled it as well.

We live through many of the same tribulations. We have to battle jealousy and anger, despair, and not measuring up. Our lives have disappointments and battles. But we know right from the moment that we recognize Christ as Savior that we are not alone. We have the living Word to comfort us. We have the Holy Spirit to intercede for us.

Reflection & Prayer

My prayer:
Lord, there will always be times when I don't feel appreciated or loved. Let me not stew in jealousy or envy. Keep me from despair. Let me turn toward the one whose love is eternal. Bring my focus to my blessings and not my disappointments. Holy Spirit, remind me to seek assurance in the living Word, the one constant and comfort. Amen.

Your Prayer:

_____

_____

_____

_____

_____

_____

_____

_____

_____

Question to Consider:

Is there a Leah in your life that you can pray for and reach out to?

_____

_____

_____

_____

_____

_____

_____

_____

_____

_____

_____

_____

_____

_____

Lord of Our Hearts

When morning came, it was Leah! And Jacob said to Laban, "What is this you have done to me? Did I not serve with you for Rachel? Why then have you deceived me?" Laban said, "This is not done in our country—giving the younger before the firstborn. Complete the week of this one, and we will give you the other also in return for serving me another seven years." Jacob did so, and completed her week. Then Laban gave him his daughter Rachel as a wife.

(Genesis 29:25–28 NRSV)

Jacob and Laban had an agreement that Jacob would work for Laban for seven years in exchange for marrying Rachel. Marriage was a contract, a business arrangement. Jacob didn't have the bride price, so seven years it was. On the wedding night, Leah is substituted for Rachel. Jacob confronts Laban, a new contract is made, and Jacob is committed to another seven years of working for Laban. I have to admire Jacob for honoring his commitment despite being taken advantage of in this arrangement. He trusted the promise of God and didn't run off with both brides at the first chance. He worked the full fourteen years.

A word about Jacob: he is a man not above trickery. First, he convinced his older twin, Esau, to sell him his birthright. Then he connived with his mother to trick his father into giving him a blessing that rightfully belonged to Esau. This bit of lying and thievery is an insight into Jacob. I see him as ruthless, yet on the way to Laban, God came to him in a dream and confirmed that Jacob would be the father of nations. Go figure! But I am having a hard time reconciling this man with the man of God's promise.

I think we face this dilemma every day. How could God bless that person? Doesn't he see that she is mistreating her children? That he is cheating on his wife?... The list is endless. Why aren't you punishing that person instead of blessing them, God? Because He knows the heart of each. He knows whether He is the Lord of their heart or something else is. He sees our heart and what is behind each of our actions. So, we will trust Him to know what is best for them as well as for ourselves, for He is the Lord of our hearts.

Reflection & Prayer

My prayer:
Father, help me to remember that my job is to worship You,
trust in You, and develop my relationship with You. I can't
see what You do in the lives of others. Their actions are
between You and them. My heart is to seek Your will in all
things and not to judge others. Amen.

Your Prayer:

_____

_____

_____

_____

_____

_____

_____

_____

_____

_____

_____

_____

Question to Consider:

Who is the Jacob in your life that you could pray for?

_____
_____
_____
_____
_____
_____
_____
_____
_____
_____
_____
_____
_____
_____
_____
_____
_____
_____

The Blessing You Have

"When morning came, there was Leah! So Jacob said to Laban, "What is this you have done to me? I served you for Rachel, didn't I? Why have you deceived me?" Laban replied, "It is not our custom here to give the younger daughter in marriage before the older one. Finish this daughter's bridal week; then we will give you the younger one also, in return for another seven years of work." And Jacob did so. He finished the week with Leah, and then Laban gave him his daughter Rachel to be his wife."

(Genesis 29:25-28 NIV)

Laban took advantage of Jacob in the marriage contract by allowing Jacob to work double what it normally would have taken to pay off a bride price. Jacob has already worked seven years to earn Rachel. Now Laban found a loophole to get another seven years out of Jacob. And it was a clever ploy because nowhere else is this custom of marrying off the elder before the younger recorded. Jacob was young and smitten, so he agreed to the terms.

Laban definitely took advantage of his daughters. I wonder how the conversation went when he informed Rachel that her sister would be entering the bridal tent instead of her. Did Rachel rail against the injustice of it? Is that why Laban agreed to allow her to marry on the promise of the contract, instead of the fulfillment?

I see in Laban a man who is fearful of poverty. His flocks had increased under Jacob, and greed seemed to take over. It took over the relationship with his daughters and caused him to worry later that Jacob had cheated him. While I was originally outraged that Laban would treat these young people so poorly, I began to pity him for allowing greed to destroy his peace. Greed tends to goad us to want more and takes our eyes off the blessings we have.

Today, look to the blessings you do have, not those you wish you had. Take count. Write them down. Let these blessings fill your heart with comfort and joy. Then go out into the world with this new joy and gratitude and be a blessing to those around you.

Reflection & Prayer

My prayer:
Lord, help me to remember that You will protect me in all circumstances. If someone takes advantage of me, help me to rest in the assurance that they will answer to You. Let me not repay evil with evil but stand on Your promises. I know that everything that happens, happens with Your knowledge. I could never strike a better deal than the one that I received when salvation was granted through Christ Jesus. I will praise You in all things. Amen.

Your Prayer:

_____

_____

_____

_____

_____

_____

_____

_____

_____

Question to Consider:

Have you ever been on the receiving end of a bad deal (work, family, purchase)? How did you respond? Would you respond differently today?

Finding Peace in the Holy Spirit

So Jacob went in to Rachel also, and he loved Rachel more than Leah. He served Laban for another seven years.

(Genesis 29:30 NRSV)

Rachel, the beloved, is worth fourteen years of contracted labor. Rachel, the sister. Rachel, the daughter. Rachel, the bargaining chip. I wonder what feelings she was going through. The excitement of her upcoming wedding and all that entailed—the feast to ready, the room to ready, nervousness about the wedding night, and the excitement. Finally, the seven years of waiting were over! Finally, she would lie with her beloved!

But no. All of Rachel's hopes are dashed with the decision of her father to send Leah as the bride. And the disappointment didn't stop there. Leah proceeded to produce son after son while Rachel waited and watched. My heart hurts for Rachel. I hope she had happiness, but I'm afraid that she was filled with sadness and envy. To make matters worse, it was the custom for a bride to live with her family until she had conceived, which in Rachel's case was at least five and a half more years. Once again, Rachel has to watch as Leah sets up house, while Rachel yearns for one. And we know so little about her, except how desperately she wanted a child. She gave her maid to Jacob for a child. She traded Leah a night with Jacob for some mandrakes, which were supposed to help conceive. Rachel finally gives birth to Joseph. And as happy as Rachel is, she right away says, "May the Lord add to me another son!" Was she now in the habit of being discontented? Had she spent so many years wrestling with her sister that she was now unable to be calm and content?

I'm sure we all know people like that. Their lives have been spent pining for something else, something better, for so long that they have forgotten how to enjoy their lives. They have become so focused on that one thing that will make them happy that they have forgotten how to be happy. They need the peace of the Holy Spirit.

Look inward today. Is there something that you, like Rachel, have been longing for so long that you have overlooked the blessings that surround you? Ask God to show you the joy before you. Let the Holy Spirit fill you with peace today.

Reflection & Prayer

My prayer:
Lord, do I have discontentment in my heart? Am I missing blessings because I am looking for something more? Fill me, Holy Spirit, with Your peace. Let me search only for more of You, Lord. Let my heart be so full of joy that I can come to You in all things. Amen.

Your Prayer:

_____

_____

_____

_____

_____

_____

_____

_____

_____

_____

Question to Consider:

When have you or someone you know experienced the disappointments that Rachel did?

_____

_____

_____

_____

_____

_____

_____

_____

_____

_____

_____

_____

_____

_____

_____

Forgive, Accept, and Let Go

I urge, then first of all that petitions, prayers, intercession and thanksgiving be made for all people—for kings and all those in authority, that we may live peaceful and quiet lives in all godliness and holiness.

(1 Timothy 2:1–2 NIV)

When I see the venom on social media toward government officials, including the president, I am saddened. How did we, as a God-fearing nation, come to the place where our differences in thought are turned to violent speech and actions? And it isn't just one political party. We no longer heed this verse to pray for all those in authority.

God doesn't ask us to pray only for those whose ideas are in agreement with our own. We are to pray for all people—for kings and all those in authority. We need to pray that world leaders be given wisdom and that they are given knowledge and compassion. After all, world leaders have a direct influence on the events that ultimately affect each of us.

That's one of the more difficult directions in the Bible. There have been presidents and government officials that I didn't vote for or like for a variety of reasons. I wanted God to change them but not me. Following this verse has revealed that it didn't matter how I felt aboutworld leaders. By not praying in earnest for their success, I was telling God that I didn't trust His hand on our nation.

How can we live peaceful and quiet lives if we are not living in godliness and holiness? If we are obeying part of the Word, the part that is easy for us to obey, then we are not truly willing to live according to God's Word. We have talked about how the Holy Spirit will guide us, and when we don't know how to pray, the Holy Spirit will intercede.

Anger with someone we don't know on a personal level or have never had personal contact with is self-defeating. Basing our like or dislike on what is reported to us by the media is basing our opinion on gossip. God wants us to put aside our anger at our brother before coming to Him.

Today forgive, accept, and let go. Holding onto anger only prevents us from growing in our relationship with the Lord. We cannot change others, however, we can pray for them. Allow God to take this burden from you so you can move on. Feel the weight being lifted from your chest as you pray and truly forgive.

Reflection & Prayer

My prayer:
Father, please forgive me for allowing hate and distrust to control my speech and actions. Cleanse my heart, Lord; and show me how to pray for our leaders in government, even if I disagree with their actions. They are accountable to You, Father, not me. Grant me wisdom and compassion toward them that I might find favor in Your eyes. Amen.

Your Prayer:

_____

_____

_____

_____

_____

_____

_____

_____

_____

_____

_____

_____

Question to Consider:

How does this verse change the way that you will pray for our leaders?

_____

_____

_____

_____

_____

_____

_____

_____

_____

_____

_____

_____

_____

_____

_____

_____

Live a Life of Joy

He has told you, O mortal, what is good; And what does the Lord require of you but to do justice, and to love kindness, And to walk humbly with your God?
(Micah 6:8 NRSV)

Micah is a prophet in the Old Testament. Here he is reminding the people of the basic behavior that God expects from them. Later, we see this echoed by Jesus in the New Testament. A "good" person will do these things because it is the minimum that is expected by society. One who loves God and wants a personal relationship with Him knows that "good" doesn't earn a place in Heaven. We can't earn a place through works, but are expected with our hearts and behavior to surpass "good."

As Christians, we want to do more than merely do what

is right when called upon. We want to apply justice to all situations—regardless of whether we like a person or not. Sometimes that part is tricky, isn't it?

I know some people make me think, "They got what is coming to them", even if in a particular situation, they were innocent. I would like to punish their previous actions, but that isn't just. Each action must be weighed in the current context and action, not on previous behavior. We can't hold anyone to a higher standard than we live (Matt. 7:2).

My sister, Tricia, is one whose heart knows justice. While I may be influenced by the emotions of a topic, she can cut right to the heart of a matter and identify the right and wrong of it. I wish I could be more like her.

While I tend to extend the benefit of the doubt to the extreme, Tricia is firm in her conviction of what is right and just. That doesn't mean that she isn't kind. She is kind and generous and loving. She reaches out to anyone that is in need, comforts them, and offers guidance. She does what God would want as second nature. If you asked her what her walk with God consisted of, I think she would probably leave out half of it because she does it without thinking. She honors God, spends time in prayer, asks for prayer, and extends love to everyone. She doesn't make a show of it. She just walks humbly with God.

As we mature in our relationship with God, this is what it will look like. While walking with God in humility, love becomes a way of life—not a constant striving to remember, but a relaxed relationship of security; a life of joy.

Reflection & Prayer

My prayer:
Lord, help me to walk with You, exhibiting justice and
kindness in a way that draws others closer to You. Amen.

Your Prayer:

_____

_____

_____

_____

_____

_____

_____

_____

_____

_____

_____

_____

_____

_____

Question to Consider:

What do you think it means to "walk humbly with God"?

Day 7

The Beauty of God's Creation

And now, dear brothers and sisters, one final thing. Fix your thoughts on what is true, and honorable and right, and pure, and lovely, and admirable. Think about things that are excellent and worthy of praise.

(Philippians 4:8 NLT)

Isn't this a lovely verse on which to end our journey together? Fixing our thoughts on those things that are excellent and praise-worthy. Turning our hearts to the pure, lovely, and admirable. Search the day, and find the true and right and honorable.

As we look around ourselves today, let's look for that which is a gift of God. Notice the birds in flight, and remember how we are more valuable to Him than a flock of sparrows. Think of the sheep in the field and how the Lamb of God was slain for you. Be like the deer that pants for water and thirst for more of the Lord. Appreciate the people you come in contact with, and recognize their beauty through the eyes of the Lord. As you brush your hair, ponder on how he knows the number of hairs on your head. Remember that one lost lamb is so precious to the shepherd that he will leave the rest of the flock to find it and bring it safely home.

God rejoices when someone repents and comes home to Him. He loves us that much! He knew your name when the world was created. He knew who you would be and why you are precious in His sight.

Acquaint yourself with the Word of God. Read it, pray through it, and rejoice in it. It was written for us to guide and encourage us throughout our days.

Reflection & Prayer

My prayer:
Father, there is so much that is wondrous and miraculous in our world! Thank You for loving me. Help me to see others through Your eyes today and appreciate them. Thank You for Your Word and Holy Spirit. Thank You for Your Son, Jesus Christ. Amen.

Your Prayer:

_____

_____

_____

_____

_____

_____

_____

_____

_____

_____

_____

_____

Question to Consider:

What do you appreciate today?

Week 8 Review

Genesis 29:20–23
Genesis 29:25–28
Genesis 29:30
1 Timothy 2:1–2
Micah 6:8
Philippians 4:8

Questions to Consider:

1. As we learned about the different people of Jacob's family, how did this lead you to think differently about the people in your life?

_____

_____

_____

2. How is God evident in the lives of this family?

_____

_____

_____

3. How is God evident in your life?

_____

_____

4. Why is it important to pray for those in authority and in government?

_____

_____

5. How does concentrating on things that are good and admirable change your perception of the world?

_____

_____

6. Review your prayers from this week. What has God said to you?

_____

_____

_____

_____

_____

_____

_____

_____

_____

Thoughts This Week

Moving Forward

I hope that you have enjoyed this devotional and are inspired to continue to study and grow in your relationship with God. Now that your reading journey is over, where do you go from here? Below are some small suggestions to help you find your next step for both new, old, and returning believers. Your success in your spiritual endeavors are in my prayers. Thank you so much for coming on this special journey with me. I pray that you feel the love of His welcoming arms with you, always.

Finding the Right Church

If you haven't found a church, I encourage you to explore churches in your area. Check them out online, learn about their beliefs, and listen to a few sermons. Consider the atmosphere: Is it welcoming? Is the leadership team approachable? Do you enjoy the worship? Did you learn something? Are you most comfortable in a large church or a small church? Let's discuss some of the advantages to each church setting. Allow God to speak to your heart about which environment feels right for you.

Large Churches

While large churches can be intimidating, they do offer many advantages: multiple services and types of worship, bookstores, cafes, child care, outreach ministries. And there will be a selection of study groups by age group, single or couples, etc. Every large church will have a way to connect with a smaller group of people who share your interests.

Small Churches

The advantages of a smaller church are being in a more intimate group, getting to know those around you quickly and, often, being a part of the growth process. Small churches need more personal involvement in terms of service and probably will have coffee time instead of a cafe, a lending table instead of a book store, and fewer services. But the sense of connection is usually more immediate.

Online Churches

You don't need to be part of a church to continue your journey but you do need a group of people who will help keep you grounded in the Word and growing. Many online churches now have e-groups that connect people of similar interests from across the world. It is important to be with others who share your beliefs, to worship, and to learn.

Find Your Spiritual Warriors

Be brave! Put the word out on among your friends and neighbors that you would like to start a Bible study. Watch how God brings others to you. Stonecroft Bible studies can be found at christianbook.com. These studies are excellent for new Christians.

Until you find another study or group you are comfortable with, check out the online Bible studies. There are many, some of which are free. An excellent resource for free Bible studies that allow you to interact with others or go solo is faithgateway.com. I have done several of their studies and they are excellent.

Seek Time Out Daily to Connect with God

I encourage you to buy a prayer journal to record your journey. I like going back to my older journals to see how I have grown and to see how my prayers were answered. This is your time to reconnect and listen to what God truly wants for you in your life. Journaling helps us to learn to discern God's voice.

Thank you for taking this walk with me, and for allowing me to share part of your journey.

Acknowledgments

I have seen acknowledgment pages and not realized how important they are to the author and those who are mentioned there. Now I do. There were many other people who loved me through the creation of this book, as they showed their enthusiasm and offered encouragement.

Family is often the staunchest supporters of any endeavor and this book was no exception. My husband, Roy, who cares for me day in and day out. I love you. My sister, Tricia Gilchrist, who has always been my biggest cheerleader, contributed invaluable advice and suggestions. My three daughters, Denise, Megan, and Kelly, who hold me accountable for walking the walk. I love you three and am very proud of the women you have become. My mom, Lee Murphy, bolstered my flagging resolve with her resolute confidence in my ability. I love you. Thank you to my spiritual barometer, my sister Kathy Cote, who confirms when I am on course.

My gratitude to the lovely women of my Bible study,

whose excitement and prayers at the prospect of this book buoyed me up: Nicole Rhyne, Megan Cowart, Lauren Wright, Lorie Schaeffer, Mayble Thomas, and Amanda Palumbo. God blessed me mightily with you!

My granddaughter, Grace, whose lovely title graces this book and whose input has been invaluable. I love you kiddo.

My dear friend, Robin Oliver, who lovingly led me to the Lord, thank you for being there every time I needed you.

This edition of His Welcoming Arms wouldn't be the lovely piece of work it is without the talents of Jessica Senesac and Kate Kropp. God continues to bless me with people like you popping into my life when least expected.

Thank you.

About the Author

Glenda Keiper was raised in an Air Force family, moving frequently throughout her life.

"Books were always my first friends at any new location. I learned to love the written word, its rhythms and patterns, meanings and origins. As a child, I would use picturesque speech to describe the car ride vistas, even when no one was listening."

Glenda Keiper had many small adventures in her life before she accepted Christ, she plans one day to share those stories when the time is right. Through years of participation and leading Bible studies, she never forgot that feeling of "being the new kid" and wrote His Welcoming Arms to help others become more comfortable with conversing with God and drawing closer to the God who loves us.

Her employment experiences were as varied as her early life. From being a stay at home mom and involved in volunteer work through the school and town committees, she learned the invaluable lesson of diplomacy. Working as a waitress refined her humility. While working as an assistant in the school system with first graders and high school students, came the refining of kindness and appreciation of their unique humor. After supervising in a large retail chain, Glenda Keiper's work career wove it's way forward. It was in her final employment that her talent and love of writing were finally allowed to emerge, through creating trainings and newsletters. Combining that exposure with her passion for studying the Word of God, this set her on the unexpected path of writing this book.

Glenda Keiper and her husband, Roy, have three daughters and nine grandchildren, scattered across the United States. Having lived the majority of her life in New England, she had promised all family members she would never live in Florida. And God laughed! Thus Bible studies and writing give her a handy excuse to avoid the sun and heat of Central Florida, where she lives with her husband and dog, Hudson.

Glenda is currently working on her first children's book, Tallulah and the Tree with the Bright Green Leaves.

"Books were always my first friends at any new location. 1 learned to love the written word, its rhyt hms and patterns, meanings and origins. As a child, 1 would use picturesque speech to describe the car ride vistas, even when no one was listening."

Thank You For Reading
His Welcoming Arms

Want to connect with the author? Follow Glenda Keiper on Facebook. She encourages her readers to reach out to her about her book or upcoming literary projects on social media. You can search "Glenda Keiper" on Facebook or scan the QR code below to follow her.